Seeing Things Politically

Other works of Interest from St. Augustine's Press

Peter Kreeft, *Socrates' Children* (in four volumes):
Ancient, Medieval, Modern, and *Contemporary*

Peter Kreeft, *Summa Philosophica*

Peter Kreeft, *Socratic Logic*

Gerhart Niemeyer, *The Loss and Recovery of Truth*

Stanley Rosen, *Essays in Philosophy* (in two volumes):
Ancient and *Modern*

Stanley Rosen, *Platonic Productions:*
Theme and Variations: The Gilson Lectures

Gabriel Marcel, *The Mystery of Being* (in two volumes):
I: *Reflections and Mystery* and II: *Faith and Reality*

Gabriel Marcel, *Man against Mass Society*

Seth Benardete, *The Archaeology of the Soul:*
Platonic Readings for Ancient Poetry and Philosophy

Philippe Bénéton, *The Kingdom Suffereth Violence:*
The Machiavelli / Erasmus / More Correspondence
and other Unpublished Documents

Rémi Brague, *On the God of the Christians:*
(and on one or two others)

Rémi Brague, *Eccentric Culture: A Theory of Western Citilization*

Roger Pouivet, *After Wittgenstein, St. Thomas*

Christopher Bruell, *Aristotle as Teacher:*
His Introduction to a Philosophic Science

Richard A. Watson, *Solipsism:*
The Ultimate Empiral Theory of Human Existence

Emanuela Scribano, *A Reading Guide to Descartes'*
Meditations on First Philosophy

Roger Scruton, *The Meaning of Conservatism*

René Girard, *A Theory of Envy: William Shakespeare*

H.D. Gerdil, *The Anti-Emile: Reflections on the Theory and*
Practice of Education against the Principles of Rousseau

Daniel J. Mahoney, *The Other Solzhenitsyn: Telling the Truth about a*
Misunderstood Writer and Thinker

Ralph C. Hancock, *Calvin and the Foundation of Modern Politics*

Joseph Cropsey, *On Humanity's Intensive Introspection*

Edward Feser, *Neo-Scholastic Essays*

Seeing Things Politically

Interviews with Bénédicte Delorme-Montini

Pierre Manent

English Translation by Ralph C. Hancock

Introduction by Daniel J. Mahoney

ST. AUGUSTINE'S PRESS
South Bend, Indiana

Originally published as Le Regard Politique:
Entretiens avec Bénédicte Delorme-Montini
© Flammarion, SA, Paris, 2010.
Translation copyright © 2015 by St. Augustine's Press

Manufactured in the United States of America

1 2 3 4 5 6   20 19 18 17 16 15

Library of Congress Cataloging in Publication Data
Manent, Pierre.
[Regard politique. English]
Seeing things politically: interviews with Benedicte
Delorme-Montini / Pierre Manent; English translation by
Ralph C. Hancock; introduction by Daniel J. Mahoney.
pages cm
Includes bibliographical references and index.
ISBN 978-1-58731-813-9 (hardback; alk. paper)
1. Political science – Philosophy. 2. Manent, Pierre – Interviews.
I. Delorme-Montini, Benedicte, interviewer. II. Title.
JA71.M26413213 2014
320.01 – dc23   2014038783

∞ The paper used in this publication meets the minimum requirements of
the American National Standard for Information Sciences Permanence of
Paper for Printed Materials, ANSI Z39.481984.

ST. AUGUSTINE'S PRESS
www.staugustine.net

CONTENTS

TRANSLATOR'S NOTE

These autobiographical and philosophical essays, in the form of expertly probing interviews, provide a superb introduction to the work of one of the most significant contemporary political philosophers and a marvelously readable perspective on the French intellectual and political arenas from the 1970s to the present. Those already familiar with Pierre Manent's work will find an indispensable reflection on his transition from the critique of modernity brilliantly represented in his earlier books (most notably *Tocqueville and the Nature of Democracy* and *The City of Man*), a critique at once original and significantly indebted to Leo Strauss, toward a perspective that emerges in his recent *The Metamorphoses of the City,* a monumental and profoundly original study that endeavors to situate modernity within the original Greek founding of the act of politics.

The autobiographical passages in this vivid and engaging work invite the reader into, first, the world of postwar France in which Manent grew up, in which he was presented with the choice between the Communist hopes of his father and the opposing power and prestige of all things American. There is also an impressive portrait of the rigors and spirit of a provincial *lycée*, where the first sparks of philosophical eros ignited in Manent's soul, and of his studies in the legendary *École Normale Superieure* in the midst of the ideological confusion associated with the ferment of 1968. The reader then is invited to an inside view of the rise of a broadly Tocquevillean school of French thought around the journal *Contrepoints* and its successor *Commentaire.*

There are a number of vivid personal vignettes offered in the book, including an affectionate one of Allan Bloom. But no portrait is more impressive than that of Manent's mentor, Raymond Aron. It was Aron who awakened Manent to the possibility of seeing things politically—and, in the first instance, of seeing political things with dispassionate clarity and rigor. Manent's sober admiration for Aron, "the perfect gentleman who experienced no need of transcendence" and who "gave each person what seemed to him best for that person without worrying about his own influence" leaves an indelible impression on the reader.

As Manent moves into an account of the origins and development of his own intellectual project, the reader is offered an intriguing introduction to his most recent and ongoing work. This work includes Manent's brilliant and original reformulation of the great question of continuity and change in the classical, Christian and modern dispensations of the Western quest to understand and to enact humanity. And it becomes clear that Manent's project is by no means of purely scholarly inspiration, but that it is rather the fruit of a sustained and penetrating engagement with the largest practical issues of our time. Our contemporary ethic of universal human rights has deep roots in our Western tradition and appears to be practically irresistible, spiritually as well as politically. However, "since the modern order is also coming up against its limits," because "public order can be built on the protection of private lives alone," it is of much more than academic interest to ask, "what objective order capable of motivating a common action" might yet be possible? This deeply practical question has informed Pierre Manent's intellectual project over four decades, and he is now unfolding it for his readers more powerfully and originally than ever. *Seeing Things Politically* is the best (and most readable and enjoyable) introduction that exists to this vital ongoing quest for clarity concerning meaningful action in the modern world.

INTRODUCTION TO *SEEING THINGS POLITICALLY*

Pierre Manent is arguably the most thoughtful and most penetrating political philosopher writing today. His clear, eloquent prose paradoxically serves to obscure his achievement: no one, it is thought, who limits himself to the language of the city and is accessible to thoughtful citizens as such can truly be deep or profound. Where some confuse abstraction and jargon with theoretical penetration, Manent pursues wisdom with grace and clarity. The breadth and depth of his work coexist with what can only be described as a humane sensibility.

The reader is in for a treat. *Seeing Things Politically* is, at one and the same time, the most accessible, charming, and thought-provoking introduction to Manent's intellectual itinerary and to the major issues of politics and political philosophy in the contemporary world. Through a series of carefully crafted responses to questions from an interviewer (or rather a collective of interviewers), Manent deftly introduces readers to his life and thought as well as to the issues that swirl around the three great poles of human existence: politics, religion, and philosophy.

We learn that Manent came from a Communist family and was for a time a youthful and convinced Marxist-Leninist. He describes that period of his life with remarkable equanimity. His father would remain a man of the Marxist Left as Manent left the Left behind for good. Father and son would quarrel about matters of deep import, but they never allowed political differences to interfere with their natural affection for each other. Manent's artful evocation of the French Communist milieu of his youth avoids both rancor and nostalgia. Yet Manent makes clear that in his maturity, from the age of seventeen or eighteen onward, he has never been a man of the Left. His great "intention" has always been "to understand what is" and not to imagine worlds that do not and cannot exist. He is an anti-utopian whose disdain for the imagination in politics, for what Tocqueville called literary politics, is real but never preachy or didactic. To see things politically is to eschew the ideological deformation of politics, the substitution of imagined "realities" for the world we are privileged to inhabit.

To see things politically, however, is not to politicize everything. This work makes clear that Manent exists in what he calls a "triangle" that consists of political reflection, philosophical inquiry, and religious truth. He is committed to each pole of human existence even as he refuses to dedicate himself to any of the poles exclusively. He engages in philosophical inquiry and affirms the truth of the Christian proposition. But the center of his reflection, the core of his intellectual ambition, is "to understand human things, and more specifically, to understand politics and political things." He is convinced that politics is the architectonic science since "the political order is what truly gives human life its form." Manent refuses to underestimate (or overestimate) the place of politics among human things. If the postmodern Left perversely 'politicizes' everything, there is a concomitant danger of saying that "real life has nothing to do with politics." Pierre Manent, in turn, restores politics to its rightful place in the human order of things.

What is apparent from the opening pages of *Seeing Things Politically* is Manent's robust confidence "in the capacity of human reason to think the human world." He has no time for facile relativism or what he calls "nihilism lite." To be clear, his is not an Enlightenment-style rationalism that erodes or eviscerates the contents of life in a dogmatic quest to explain them away. Rather, he has confidence in the power of the soul to think politically, to grasp trans-historical truth and to affirm an enduring phenomenology of the human world. Manent is not only immune to the temptation of nihilism, he is anti-totalitarian to his core. With wit and some consternation, he describes the assortment of totalitarian and proto-totalitarian ideologies that dominated the elite École Normale Supérieure when he arrived there in 1967. It was truly "a ship of fools." Having left Marxism-Leninism behind, Manent was not at all inclined to turn to Maoism or Trotskyism, or any other fanatical excuses for abolishing human reason and human liberty. While having a lively interest in Marx and Nietzsche as thinkers or philosophers of the utmost importance, he knew that they bore some responsibility for the totalitarian scourges of the twentieth century. Coming of age with the '68 generation, Manent forthrightly rejected what has been called "the thought of '68."

Manent mentions that Hannah Arendt's *The Origins of Totalitarianism* was an early influence on him. He read the book in the library of the École Normale Supérieure and admired Arendt's capacity to philosophize profoundly about a human experience—totalitarianism—that was central to the twentieth century. He would later find much to criticize in Arendt's work. But *Origins* had an enduring influence on Manent and helped inform his principled rejection of totalitarianism. It, also, shaped his growing appreciation that political philosophy must have the courage to speak to and form judgments about political experience, especially an experience as fundamental as the totalitarian assault on the bodies and souls of human beings.

Manent makes much of the human soul's capacity for conversion, a theme we will turn to later in this presentation. For now, let us say that his rejection of Communism went hand-in-hand with a double conversion. The first was to Catholicism. Here, the great influence was his lycée teacher in Toulouse, Louis Jugnet. Jugnet was a talented professor of philosophy who taught—and taught well—the required curriculum of philosophical studies. But he was also a Thomist of conviction who conveyed to Manent the vital lesson that there was something *to know* in religion, that it was not reducible to sentiment or to some private realm of interiority. Manent's conversion to Catholicism, as a result, was rooted in intellectual conviction more than feeling or sentiment. He was convinced that Christianity knew the truth about man, that it revealed the truth of the created natural order even as it captured the human soul in all its grandeur and misery.

A truly beautiful section of Part II of this work addresses Pierre Manent's relationship to his two greatest teachers and influences, Raymond Aron and Leo Strauss. Manent's encounter with Aron might be called his second conversion, his conversion to political reason or practical wisdom. The greatness of Aron is difficult to convey to a contemporary American audience. He was a prolific scholar who wrote over forty-five books in his lifetime, with dozens more being published posthumously. He wrote on the philosophy of history, German sociology, the great questions of peace and war, the politics of the twentieth century. He was influenced by Max Weber (although Weber's dalliance with Nietzschean nihilism and power politics was completely alien to him), the political Aristotle, Thucydides, Montesquieu and Tocqueville. His final work on Clausewitz as a philosopher of war is a masterpiece, a work of exquisite interpretation that also serves as a defense of political reason against the twin extremes of pacifism and bellicosity. But above and beyond all this, he was, Manent argues, an "educator of the European city." For fifty years, he helped educate and inform moderate and conservative opinion against the illiberal extremes of Left and Right. He was the antithesis of Sartre who opined irresponsibly about politics without knowing much about it. In a work like *The Opium of The Intellectuals* (1955) he took Sartre and other *Marxisant* and fellow-traveling intellectuals to task for their indulgence to totalitarianism. He thought there was something *to know* in politics, and he rejected the facile path of those "beautiful souls" who were committed to "imaginary principalities" put forward by leftist theorists and ideologues. For Manent, Aron was nothing less than a Ciceronian orator or rhetor, "a man in the public square, who speaks with authority and competence and eloquence of public affairs." Manent admires the writings and essays of Aron. But most of all, he saw in Aron a man who embodied Aristotelian *phronesis*, someone who lived the life of deliberation, prudence, and judgment. And Aron's gift of speech—that rare Ciceronian gift—allowed him to defend European liberty in an unrivalled way in an age when it was under assault from ideology and, more subtly, from the sentimentality and humanitarianism of a new European civil religion. Against the murderous appeal to ideology and the groundless evocation of humanitarian values, Aron followed the path of reasonable choice and tough-minded moderation. Manent was Aron's assistant at the Collège de France and developed an unusually close friendship with a man forty-four years his elder. As his frequent mentions of Aron in this book make clear, his admiration for the great French political thinker has only grown over the years.

It was Raymond Aron who first recommended that Manent read Leo Strauss's *Natural Right and History*. Manent had come to feel the need for some horizon beyond the political, a transcendental measure by which politics could be judged. Aron thought that Strauss could help provide that philosophical perspective on politics. Manent would never leave Aron behind but he would henceforth explore politics and political philosophy with many of the new insights provided by Strauss. Manent was impressed by the dialectical method central to ancient philosophy, the searching critique of Machiavellian modernity limned by Strauss, and the recovery of the citizen's perspective as the starting point of all political debate and disputation. Above all, he admired Strauss's anti-historicism, his denial that thought was simply the product of the society from which it arose. Strauss's understanding of the "art of writing," so controversial in scholarly circles, served to liberate modern man "from the 'sociological point of view' that tends to determine the way we look at our humanity." Strauss allowed one to see that it was possible to be an unbeliever in the age of faith and a believer in a secular age.

But Manent has never simply been a "Straussian." To begin with, he confesses to never having made much sense of the Straussian idea of the "philosopher." If the Aristotelian or Tocquevillian political scientist "sees not differently but further than the parties" (a position fully endorsed by Strauss), the Straussian philosopher ultimately aims to transcend the moral and political plane altogether. He aims to separate himself from the human realm, proclaiming his self-sufficiency and exposing the "contradictions" in the lives dedicated to morality, religion, and politics. What is more, Manent does not find the Straussian interpretation of Socrates to be compelling or convincing. This Socrates leaves us with too much *aporia* and not enough respect for the common sense origins and evidences of morality and politics. Manent's work, in contrast, is marked by a striking fidelity to the moral "contents of life." He opposes any vision of philosophizing that dissolves, or tends to dissolve, the goods of life. Following the French Catholic poet-philosopher Charles Péguy, he affirms the dignity of the "temporal," of the created natural order. This affirmation of the temporal informs his understanding of both philosophy and religion. If he cannot abide an understanding of philosophy that leaves the human realm behind or that is too convinced of its own self-sufficiency or autarky, he will not affirm an order of grace that demotes or neglects the natural order. Half-Thomist and half-Straussian, he believes that both philosophy and religion must do justice to the full range of human experience. Both philosophy and religion must respect the pagan virtues, especially the cardinal virtues: courage, temperance, justice, and prudence. They must not negate them in the name of an understanding of philosophy that severs intellectual virtue from moral virtue or an account of the transcendent that looks down with contempt on the temporal.

We have already mentioned Manent's conversion to the Catholic faith. In *Seeing Things Politically* he expresses a paradox at the heart of his reflection on the theological-political problem. On the one hand, Christianity "knows the truth about man," it is nothing less than the "crystal of every desired truth." On the other hand, Christianity has a hard time doing justice to the full range of human experience, especially the political experience of man. The Moderns—Machiavelli, Hobbes, Rousseau—were not completely wrong about the political incompetence of Christianity. Christianity is not politically 'operational' and there is no such thing as a Christian political theology. And some Christians were tempted to radically depreciate the temporal world and the virtues that were attendant to it. Manent quotes a jarring remark from Péguy: "the error of the devout party is to believe that they are people of grace because they lack the strength to be of nature."

Does this mean that Manent despairs of the capacity of religion to do justice to human experience, including the political experience of man? The answer is no. But he will not rest content with the pieties and evasions of the devout party. He must live within the aforementioned triangle and do everything he can to remain faithful to the three great poles of human experience. In a capital passage in part II of this work, Manent reflects on how the Bible "brings together fidelity to human experience and commitment to a religious perspective." In the Old Testament, especially the *Psalms*, the two "are strangely, paradoxically reconciled." One finds directly and immediately "human experience in its greatest ignorance of God and, mysteriously a presence of God that does not impinge upon, that does not cover up the authenticity of experience." Manent writes:

> The text of the *Psalms* is particularly overwhelming because, in a chaotic and popular language, it maintains a balance that the greatest religious minds have not been able to maintain so perfectly. This is a text in which we find a human being who complains, who cries out in pain, who protests, who wants to kill his enemies, who is afraid of dying, who is sick, and, mysteriously, at the same time, we find an experience of something radically different from all human experience but which does not prevent this experience from being lived and described in its whole truth, in its nakedness. This, in a way, is an argument for the 'revealed character' of the Bible, in that it includes texts that manage to hold together what no human being can hold together within the limits of human expression.

What the Bible achieves in an unparalleled way, the believer is obliged to imitate however imperfectly and haltingly. Commitment to a religious perspective and fidelity to human experience allows one to do justice to the conscience, that is to the soul's invisible reflection of the moral law as well as to those "visible" pagan virtues that Christians are so often tempted to leave behind. To live the theological-political problem is to live a tension that cannot be resolved but only mediated by the twin workings of nature and grace. And through the promise of "communion," the great human task of "putting things in common," believers and unbelievers alike experience nature's grace, the sacred ties or bonds that allow us to experience the sacred in the temporal. As Manent's example attests, one can think politically about religion without denying religious truth.

Seeing Things Politically also provides an excellent introduction to Manent's work as a scholar and political philosopher. We see that his engagement with the theological-political problem has been coextensive with a forty-year engagement with the "Machiavellian imperative." Manent's early work shows a particular sensitivity to the "modern difference"—the way that modernity has transformed human consciousness by creating a world where the flight from evil took primacy over the search for the Good. Manent's interpretations of Machiavelli, Hobbes, Montesquieu, Rousseau, and Tocqueville, among others, have allowed us to better appreciate the explicit and emphatic modern rejection of classical and Christian wisdom. Manent's early writings display something of an anti-modern sensibility (although his approach to politics always affirmed the best liberal conservative wisdom and thus eschewed every form of extremism). He writes with admiration about Tocqueville's efforts to describe the new democratic man who is the end-product of the modern "democratic revolution." That "democratic man" is always in danger of succumbing to individualism—the disassociation of human life—and he is haunted by the specter of "democratic despotism." In his 1982 book *Tocqueville and the Nature of Democracy*, Manent more or less endorsed Tocqueville's phenomenology of the democratic world. His admiration for Tocqueville's achievement is undiminished, even if he now thinks that Tocqueville ultimately exaggerated the effects of the "democratic revolution." This reader happens to believe that Manent's revised judgment on Tocqueville goes too far in the other direction: Tocqueville, after all, always believed that the "nature" of democracy could be moderated and even elevated by what he called the "art of liberty." He was not a historicist in the strict sense of the term, since he affirmed the autonomy of politics and an elevated place for human and political choice. Tocqueville also believed that democratic man can be understood only in his dialectical relationship to "aristocratic man," to the man that came before him. The latter point, I should add, is one that Manent freely acknowledges in *Seeing Things Politically*.

The present-day Manent does not deny the "modern difference"—the myriad transformations brought about by the new human motives (self-interest, anti-theological ire, the bourgeois desire for safety and comfort)—that was unleashed by modernity. In fact, he is currently the most incisive critic of the new European civil religion, the religion of humanitarianism, that reigns in late modernity. But Manent now places modernity in a broader historical framework beginning with the Greek city, the city that replaced the rule of unquestioned laws passed down from the ancestors with politics, with the realm of action and deliberation *par excellence*. He is increasingly preoccupied with the paradox of a modernity that used to be capable of generating great actions—the (partial) break with the classical and Christian inheritance, the building of the modern state, the great democratic revolutions in France and America—that now chooses to pursue inaction and passivity as a matter of principle. Modernity was a great *political* project. Now it is plagued by the twin currents of depoliticization and deChristianization. The old religion and the old nations are on the defensive in Europe and the new West—still dialectically dependent on the old European inheritance—is on the verge of giving up the ghost.

Much of Manent's recent work has centered on the exploration of the "political forms" that supplement and give life to political regimes: the city, empire, and nation among them. Manent had first explored this theme in his 1987 work *An Intellectual History of Liberalism*. But he has more recently returned to it with rare depth and penetration in books such as *La raison des nations* and *The Metamorphoses of the City: An Essay on the Western Dynamic*. The Greek city, particularly Athens, was the birthplace of politics. It was the engine that propelled subsequent Western political development. The Greek city was the "smallest human association capable of self-government." The empire, on the other hand, "is the most extensive possible assembling under a single sovereign." Rome was the home of the 'impossible' transformation of the city into its antithesis, empire. Rome also became the home of the "Roman Church," an invisible empire that reigned over the souls of men. In *The Metamorphoses of the City* Manent highlights the grandeur of Cicero who heroically tried to philosophize in this new situation. Faithful to Plato and Aristotle (as well as to the best of the Stoic tradition), Cicero nonetheless introduced certain themes and doctrines "that we are tempted to associate with properly modern political philosophy." He defined the magistrate as the one who "bore the public person," he "defined the function of the political order as that of protecting property, which was a definition equally foreign to the Greeks." For fifteen centuries he was a theoretical guide to European political reflection even if no one was able to give his ideas an "operational form." This long "Ciceronian moment" coexisted with disorder in the West—only the formation of the modern nation in the high Middle Ages and the early modern period would give Europeans a serviceable political form. Manent is that rare Catholic thinker who does not romanticize the Middle Ages or confuse the beauty and transcendent splendor of the cathedrals with a cogent and coherent political life.

Much of Manent's more explicitly political work centers around the study of the nation as a political form. The nation is the fourth great political form. It comes after the city, empire, and Church. Manent insists that there can be no democracy without nations since the nation gives democracy a body—a territorial framework—that allows self-government to flourish. "If nation states are in the process of disappearing in Europe, it is the matrix of European life that is being undone." The indefinite expansion of Europe—its seeming obliviousness to territory and boundaries— is based on the mistaken assumption that humanitarian "values" are somehow sufficient to build a political community. Instead of building a new political form, "something radical that has rarely been accomplished in history," the European democracies have established projects and institutions—so-called "European" institutions—that "do not take into account the question of political form, or even the question of regime." They wallow in a new humanitarian civil religion that ignores the crucial prerequisites of democratic self-government. But necessity is a harsh teacher. "Sooner or later Europeans will have to remember the political condition of humanity." Manent reminds his fellow Europeans that they will still have ample moral and political resources for the strengthening of the European spirit. The "old nations" and the "old religion" are there for the taking. Contemporary Europeans ignore them at their own peril.

Some of the richest pages in *Seeing Things Politically* deal with the distinctive character of the West. The West is, according to Manent, that civilization that has discovered the remarkable powers of the human soul. "The indeterminate but urgent" task of the West has always been the production of *something in common*. Rather than slavishly following the gods or the ancestors, rather than postulating a law that demanded "simple obedience," the West has aimed to conjugate the imperatives of truth and community through free political life. It has recognized that the question of justice is inseparable from the "question concerning the truth of mankind, concerning his 'nature' or his 'essence.'" The loss of confidence in reason's capacity to know the nature of man or to "put things in common" in a political community worthy of free human beings is evidence of a civilizational crisis, of a loss of faith in reason and the human soul.

In a beautiful passage near the end of the book, Manent discusses conversion as one of the human possibilities distinctive to the West. Conversion "consists in the possibility of becoming completely different while staying the same." "It takes great confidence in the soul to accept this possibility and to take up this adventure." The pagan and Christian West both affirmed the possibility of conversion, of a turning of the soul to truth and the source of being. Those non-Western religions and cultures such as Islam that punish apostasy, who deny the legitimacy and even the possibility of conversion, do not understand the full powers of the human soul. They dilute the drama of the soul and deny a liberty, that of conversion, that is essential to self-knowledge and free human life.

This book has the added benefit of an "Epilogue" on "Knowledge and Politics" in which Pierre Manent lays out the case for a "practical philosophy" that moves away from vacuous talk about values and that roots deliberation and action in the cardinal virtues of courage, temperance, justice, and prudence. Manent here acknowledges the tensions between the political and Christian virtues. But he warns us against the temptation of saying good-bye to Aristotle and the Gospels. Deliberation and reasonable choice lie before us exactly as they lay before Pericles and St. Paul. The illusion of a science of History—of inexorable necessity—is really a choice for inaction, for resigning ourselves to a spiritually flaccid condition where we neither fight nor love our enemies. Manent pleads against the "disarmament" of the human soul and the erosion of the human and political virtues that have made the West the West. This essay is a perfect complement, and a fitting conclusion, to *Seeing Things Politically.*

Pierre Manent provides a powerful and persuasive defense of "practical philosophy" against the regnant European civil religion and all those intellectual currents that deny reasonable choice. His critique of theoretical modernity admirably avoids anti-modern ire. His thoughtful engagement with Leo Strauss draws on the best currents of Strauss's thought while avoiding sectarian dogmatism and a unilateral emphasis on the "philosopher." His treatment of Raymond Aron allows us to better appreciate true political greatness and the requirements of political reason. His study of political forms is an essential contribution to comparative politics and political theorizing. And most importantly, this little intellectual and spiritual masterpiece reveals that the West, at its best, is informed by confidence in human reason and the powers of the soul. May it inspire a similar confidence in its readers.

Daniel J. Mahoney
August 1, 2014

SEEING THINGS POLITICALLY

PIERRE MANENT, WHAT IS YOUR INTELLECTUAL PROJECT? WHAT, FINALLY, ARE YOU LOOKING FOR?

I want to understand—or rather I desire to understand. Obviously, this answer seems at once emphatic and flat, but, in reality, I believe it is not banal, because of late the desire to understand has manifestly been abandoned in favor of another desire that has acquired great prestige, that is, the desire to create. Today the human ambition is to be a creator. There are great creators, middling creators, and small creators, but everyone has the ambition to be a creator. The human faculty that receives all the praise is the imagination. Now it happens that I have no imagination; I am not an artist, and I have no ambition to create. What I want instead is to understand.

What do I want to understand? What *is*. And it seems to me, once again, that to understand what is, is not something that stirs the ambitions of our contemporaries. They are more interested, one might say, in what is not. Rousseau, the great master of the moderns in this matter, said, "Only what is not is beautiful." For me, fundamentally, the opposite is true: only what *is* interests me. And this is perhaps the reason why, at least since I became an adult, I have not been able to be on the left, because the left prefers to imagine a society that *is not*, and I have always found the society that *is* more interesting than the society that might be.

My intention is, therefore, to understand what is. Of course, one has to limit one's ambition: I address neither what is in the stars, nor what is in the depths of the sea, nor what exists at the subatomic level, because everything to do with the natural sciences escapes me completely. My ambition is to understand human things, and more specifically, to understand politics and political things. Not because I see political things as a subset of the human things that interest me, but because the political order is what truly gives human life its form. Political things are the cause of human order or disorder. In brief, to respond to your question as directly as possible, my only ambition is to understand politics or political things.

This ambition presupposes a reevaluation of the place of politics among human things. We tend to oscillate between underestimating and overestimating its place. We overestimate when we politicize everything by saying "everything is political"; we underestimate when we say "real life has nothing to do with politics." So I seek to discern the true role of politics in the ordering of the human world.

Is this quest equivalent to the task of political philosophy? Are philosophy, political philosophy, and political science three different ways to apprehend the human world?

I have obviously never considered myself a sociologist or an anthropologist, nor as well a historian or a philosopher. Truly, I would care very little to be considered or recognized as a philosopher. This is, first, because I am reasonably modest, and also because my intellectual life has always been drawn toward a subject rather than guided by a discipline. This subject thus concerns the problems of politics. And so I am, in a way, open to anything that sheds light on these problems.

For someone interested in these questions, Machiavelli, for example, is one of the most penetrating authors there is, but his status as a philosopher is uncertain. I might add, without boasting, because it's true, that a significant part of what is supposed to interest philosophers interests me very little. And there are certain works of the modern philosophical canon that I do not admire as would be expected of a person of some learning. Unlike the works of Greek philosophy that are all muscle, blood, and nerves and that, moreover, have a sweet and luminous surface, most of the great modern works are pervaded by and, in my opinion, stuffed with and disfigured by a connective tissue of abstractions. These abstractions are perhaps essential to what one calls profundity, but then this is a profundity that I am resolved not to buy at such a price.

In any case, the most fashionable modern philosophy has little to do with politics. Inversely, the philosophical rank of the most interesting political authors is uncertain. Montesquieu is a political author of marvelous discernment, but he is not in the canon of great philosophers. Since in my view human life takes shape and presents itself first in political life, I have always sought the true first philosophy from political authors, whether they are certified philosophers or not, without worrying much about their calling card or about their official function in the various camps of knowledge.

The difficult question for me, and one I would love to know how to answer, is that of the relation between, on the one hand, this first philosophy of the human order, an order that takes the form of political order, and what on the other hand we would call political science. The author who for me has the most authority on these questions, that is, Aristotle, treats the questions that interest me under the rubric of political science. Only very rarely does he use the term political philosophy and then it is to designate the dialectical treatment of difficulties that surround the question of political justice. I would be quite content to leave it at what the master has written, but I retain a certain perplexity. When I try to give an account of the passage from one political form to another, with the help of ancient and modern historians, of philosophical and literary works, and of religious and theological texts, under what rubric shall I place this inquiry. This inquiry is subject to no disciplinary protocol, and yet, it does not proceed at random, or at least I hope not. I have no clear and satisfying answer to this question. Let's say that, since I aim to understand politics, if I practice the discipline, then it is political science. All these words are equivocal, but my intention is mainly to attain a political science.

If there is a political science, that means that one can know something of politics. But what do we know of politics?

I believe that we know much about politics. We know much, if we are willing to make the effort to know it. Since, as I have said, it is in politics that we see the main thrust of human things, we can know much about human things if we make the necessary effort. There is a science of human things. This is what I believe, and there are very few who believe it. Our contemporaries think that there is obviously a science of nature, the proof being that technology, which is based on natural science, produces extraordinary things. But people take it as given that there exists no science of human things properly speaking. Just ask not only the legendary man in the street, but even most specialists in human and social sciences. What will they tell you? They will say, "as far as human things go, there are finally only points of view or perspectives, the different perspectives depending on all kinds of factors, which depend upon historical or familial circumstances, on each individual's values, and which also depend, of course, on the scientific discipline by means of which one intends to grasp the perspectives." Therefore, if one wishes to establish a political science, this must be done in opposition to this overwhelming opinion—because this is at once a popular opinion and the expert opinion—according to which, where human things are concerned, there are only diverse perspectives that cannot be gathered into a unified science. It is necessary to demonstrate the objective character of this knowledge concerning which most of our contemporaries have the greatest doubts.

This contemporary "perspectivism" contributes to what can be called nihilism, because the definition of nihilism, or one of its possible definitions, is the loss of confidence in human reason. We have no confidence in the capacity of human reason to grasp the human world. This conviction that reason gives no access to human things has now become the most widespread opinion under the name of relativism. Call it nihilism lite.

We contemporaries, therefore, do not believe that we can understand human things, and consequently, we do not love human things; this is the other aspect of nihilism. We do not love them because we cannot understand them. It seems to us that we cannot understand them and thus, because of this distance between human things and ourselves, there cannot be this friendship for human life that we cannot, after all, help but desire.

How do you explain this nihilism? How did we come to this distrust of reason and this disaffection from human things?

Several factors might be mentioned, but to consider the one that is most relevant to our discussion, I believe that, if we are in this situation, this is, in a sense, because of the withering away of authentic political science. Whether we say "authentic political science" or "authentic political philosophy," the point is that it has virtually disappeared in the latest period of our history.

Take the 20th century. One would have to admit that this century saw some events of considerable importance for political life: great wars and great revolutions. And at the same time we saw the near-disappearance of political science and even of political philosophy. Or perhaps we should invert the terms: while the 20th century saw the near-disappearance of political science or political philosophy, it gave rise to an extreme politicization of human life, especially in Europe. I am struck by the coincidence of these two phenomena: totalitarian systems leading to an unprecedented politicization of human life, a politicization that has never been experienced to such a degree in human history; and, at the same time, mankind in the 20th century has been stripped of the basic means for thinking through what is happening. If a man like Stalin was able to present himself simply as the "General Secretary," and if, at the same time, it was possible for him to be considered a paragon of humanity and the father of the arts and sciences, this is to some degree because, in 20th century Europe, we had become incapable of using a word: the word "tyrant," or the word "tyranny." So at a time when the most horrible tyrannies in history were taking hold, the word and the notion of tyranny escaped us. This politicization in the absence of political thought or of a minimally competent political science is, I believe, one of the factors in the disorder of the century.

Along the same lines, if we keep in mind the relationship between understanding and friendship, we see that the period of totalitarianisms joins together a failure of understanding with hatred. This failure and this hatred are linked, because in this world that we are unable to grasp, this world that we are unable to come to terms with intellectually, this world in which we cannot recognize a tyrant for what he is, passions are unleashed without any means to clarify them. Let me repeat: this horrible unleashing of totalitarian passions is linked in an essential way with the incapacity of human beings of the 20th century to think through what they were doing. This is unprecedented. Never, I think, in Western history has there been such an incapacity to understand and articulate what was being done as in the 20th century. This is, I think, the major factor behind the extreme movements of the century, which is for me a powerful motive to try to rediscover the foundations of a political science or political philosophy.

One last point to confirm the preceding: it has to tell us something that the great philosophers of the century, or those who are considered the great philosophers of the century—Heidegger, Husserl, Bergson, Wittgenstein—had so little to say concerning politics. If you gather what the greatest philosophers of the century wrote about politics, it is truly disappointing! They have so little to say about politics. I mentioned Heidegger: as you know, when he speaks of public affairs, it would have been better for him to keep silent.

What can be the foundations of a new political science in an age of relativism?

Very early I had the sense that it was necessary to regain confidence in political knowledge, and thus to rediscover or establish the foundations of political science. Of course, the difficulty is that, however desirable this science may be, it is far from certain that it is possible: there are many things that are desirable but not possible. Is this science possible? I did not arrive one morning telling myself: "the world has lost political science as it must have it, so I am going to produce this political science." No, but still I observed, and anyone can make the same observation, that not so long ago, in a world close to ours, there was a very relevant political science. I am thinking of the first half of the 19th century, when Europe, and France in particular, was emerging from the convulsions of the French Revolution and of the wars of Empire and all that followed.

If we compare the revolutionary experience and the experience of totalitarianism, there are similarities: great convulsions, great wars, the phenomena of terror, devastations and massacres. But look at how France came out of this terrible period, dominated by the "murder machine," as Châteaubriand said. It comes out with the capacity for a marvelous literature, a splendid poetry, and for the analysis of modern society and of modern politics characterized by a precision, an elegance and the scope that we have admired since the rediscovery of Benjamin Constant, Guizot, and Tocqueville. The society that went through the French Revolution and the Empire and that was born of convulsions and violence, was a society capable of self-understanding. We are thus aware of a great political science linked with a great political experience, which is the experience of France and of Europe at the moment the democracies were established in the early 19th century.

Let us return to the question, is this desirable science possible? Yes, we have the proof that it is possible! Once again: France emerged from devastations and from wars with an understanding of what had happened that is wholly admirable and that still represents for us the greatest body of political science from which we can benefit immediately. One might call it "the liberal political science of democratic society." The formula is a little long but it is precise. From this point, we can envision reconstituting a political science, because this was our last great science of a great experience. This is what I felt and I went instinctively in this direction. In any case, this was not a personal project, but the project of what I would call my generation: each in his own way, we all moved toward this available political science, while the prestige of communism finally crumbled.

When you describe your project, you always insist on the link between science and experience. And you are skeptical concerning the usefulness of methodology, to say the least. Would you say that your approach aims to establish a science without methodology?

You are trying to ruin what remains of my career at the University! But it's true. Precisely because I have such reservations concerning the methodological project with its proliferation of precautions and prolegomena, I would not even propose a methodology of the absence of methodology. So what do I do? I try to find that point or that zone where the authentic political sciences—there have been at least two—are articulated in connection with the great political experiences.

We have at our disposition at least two authentic political sciences. One is the ancient science, which is mainly Greek, which gives an account of the former experience of the city, and the modern and liberal science that is divided into two segments: before and after the modern political revolution. Before the revolution, during the 17th and 18th centuries, the architects of liberalism elaborated the principles of a new order, an order and a set of principles that are still ours and that are summed up in the idea of "the rights of man." After the revolution, in the first half of the 19th century, there is a reflection on the best ways to put the principles to work, and there is an analysis of the effects of the new order, sometimes unexpected and unwanted.

There is a very obvious difference between the ancient cycle and the modern cycle. For the Greeks, experience came before theory. Plato and Aristotle were lucky! When they analyzed the city, it was at the end of its development. It was possible to sum it up. Our scientific situation does not seem so favorable. Among the moderns, political science comes, as I have said, before and after experience. Liberal political science, taken as a whole that goes from Hobbes or Locke to Tocqueville, is at once a constructive project and an evaluative description. Since this project is incomplete, since we always intended to "democratize democracy," our experience also seems to be incomplete. How then can our science be anything but provisional? This is why many among us wait for a future democracy to tell us what we should think of present democracy. I think that we can, and therefore that we must, be more ambitious. We are probably as advanced in the modern democratic cycle as the Greeks were in the democratic cycle of the city at the time of Aristotle, and certainly more advanced than they were at the time of Plato. We have no excuse for not trying with all our strength to understand, and thus to evaluate, where we stand.

I just mentioned ambition, scientific ambition. If I let myself get carried away in invoking what would be the extreme limit of my ambition—you are inviting me to do this, aren't you?—I would say that I would like to be capable finally of replacing the two great political cycles of the West, including, of course, the very long period that separates and joins them, in a *histoire raisonnée* based upon this single hypothesis: man is a political animal. To lay out our whole *history* starting from our political *nature*—that is what I would like to show and to make comprehensible.

PART ONE: APPRENTICESHIPS

CHILDHOOD AND POLITICS

When did you first become interested in politics?

My interest in politics was extremely precocious. I feel like saying that it started when the Americans arrived in my grandmother's garden. I was seven years old. It was a summer day. I was working with my father, very happy to be a big boy and to help him with whatever he was doing. Moved by the happiness of the moment, I said something to him that I must have heard at school: how the Americans seemed like such terrific guys. My father's response was so scathing that I still remember how it shocked me and how disappointed I was. This was my point of entry into political experience. The feelings that I wanted to experience concerning the Americans were so vigorously rebuffed that I understood very obscurely but very powerfully that there were subjects that incite violent disagreement, and that my father's opinion could be very different from the opinion of my little friends. In brief, I had the experience of the conflictual character of political life, my first experience of political passion, and I believe that this realization that there was something conflictual that often involved Americans was not a bad point of entry into politics!

Of course, I quickly espoused my father's perspective with all the passion of which a child is capable. Although this is mostly forgotten now, the rivalry between the United States and the Soviet Union focused on the conquest of space. And so, as a little boy, I was passionately interested in this rivalry over space. Eventually I managed to become fairly knowledgeable in the art of putting satellites in orbit; I knew how to distinguish among the various missiles, I knew the throw weights of American and Soviet missiles, and I was capable of discussing various technical matters. I must have been eight or nine years old.

So your political education began at that age?

Yes, I think I can say that my political education started at this very precocious age because I was already experiencing some of the main feelings associated with politics, particularly the passionate desire for victory, the desire to be on the side of the winners, which at that time accounted for much of my attraction to the Soviet Union. On this point, I have a memory that may seem to you of little interest and purely anecdotal. But for me it relates to something important, namely the experience of temptation, the temptation of treason. In this rivalry between the Soviet Union and United States, each side tended to claim its own advantage. Obviously I was persuaded that it was the Soviet Union that was in the lead. But one day, the United States put into orbit a satellite that was heavier than those the Soviet Union had put into orbit. This raised a serious question for me: was my champion going to be beaten? And I remember very well the temptation that arose that took the form of this thought: what, finally, obliges me to stay on the side of the Soviet Union? If the Americans are stronger, why wouldn't I change my champion? I really experienced this feeling. For St. Augustine, there were the pears in the neighbor's field. For me, the experience of temptation was political, and it consisted in the temptation to change sides in order to be with the winners. Fortunately, it soon became clear that what the Americans presented as a satellite that was heavier than the Soviet satellite was really only the third stage of the missile, and that they had, therefore, cheated and that I could return to being a faithful little soldier of the Soviet camp. That was the end of my temptation.

What would have to be called my passion for the Soviet Union lasted a good many years. This passion has been described in a number of memoirs, the authors speaking of themselves or people close to them. In any case, I have a very vivid memory that everything that was Soviet, or even simply Russian, had a certain aura about it, a golden glow, and truly belonged to a sacred space. To hear a few words from Khrushchev in Russian on the radio was a moment full of emotion. I am struck, in retrospect, by another point, that is, the contemplative character of this engagement with all its passion. I say contemplative because there was never any question for us in those days of going to see what lay behind the Iron Curtain. There was no question of visiting any country in the Soviet camp, even though we were passionately attached to that camp. There is something there that strikes me as very strange. Later, I went to spend three weeks in the Soviet Union, and my father much later still, just before the end of the Soviet Union.

Along the way, for the child that I was still, this experience of political passion gradually took an intellectual turn. I was growing up and, in any case, it was perhaps my nature. So I read the bracing novels of the collection *"In the Land of Stalin,"* of which I still have fond memories.

Do you have any definite memories of these readings?

Yes, for example, I often read and much liked Boris Polevoy's *A Real Man*, which I imagine is almost unknown today. It was a story, barely enhanced but plainly heroic, of a Soviet pilot during the war, whose plane was shot down and who had lost both his legs and who, with prosthetic legs and rehabilitation proved himself capable of again taking command of a plane and shooting down German aircraft. And here's another great memory: Nicolai Ostrovsky's *How the Steel was Tempered*—but this is no doubt much better known.

Then there were the books of *Social Editions* from my father's library; these were the school of my first reflections. These included classic texts with presentation and notes as well as works on contemporary subjects. Of course they conformed to the ideological orthodoxy of the Communist Party, but they were rather well done and I found them interesting. I read Roger Garaudy, Georges Cogniot, and Jean Kanapa. It is odd to consider that these names that now evoke what was most ideological and narrow in the French Communist movement represented, as it happened, my first intellectual education.

So were your whole family Communists? And your parents' friends?

We certainly lived in a politically homogeneous milieu. In our little familiar circle, everyone was of the left, even if my father was the only communist. There were sometimes vigorous discussions with socialist friends, of course, but these remained debates among leftists. One hardly ever met anyone of the right. We were aware that there was such a thing, but it was, if you will, like the Borneo lizard: it is known to exist but you never see one. Later, by the way, I brushed up against social milieus where the opposite was true, where people had never come across a leftist. And as for communists, such people would have performed an exorcism on the house if one had passed through. My itinerary thus, in a way, allowed me to go from a homogeneous milieu that I knew from the inside to at least encounter or get to know a bit some homogeneous milieus from the other side. Thus, I accept political partisanship with considerable equanimity. Partisanship and even political paranoia strikes me as perfectly ordinary, perfectly natural. I am, then, to conclude, just as passionate as I was at nine years old, but I am just fine with someone not seeing things my way.

I must insist on one point. Our milieu was politically homogeneous, but friendships were independent of politics. We were close friends there who were precisely not "comrades from the cell." This strikes me in retrospect. It indicates that, though there was much passion, there was no fanaticism.

You say that you lived in a politically homogeneous milieu. Was the public school you attended also leftist?

To say that I lived in a politically homogeneous milieu is true of family and friends. But in the primary school and the *lycée* (the secondary school which then included the *college* or middle school) the groups were mixed together; my fellow students were often Catholics, and my teachers as well. And as you might expect, I demonstrated vehemently for them that there was no God.

This is another feature that surprises me in retrospect: I do not recall that my very confident and very explicit communism ever provoked the slightest rejection, or even the slightest unpleasant reaction, neither among my schoolmates nor among my teachers, before or with whom I spoke without hesitation. And yet this was an era of strong ideological conflicts and often of serious political crises. This tells me that the *lycée* Pierre-de-Fermat in Toulouse was a place of high civilization. Of course, I was only a child, but still everyone, including the children, always considered me with benevolence.

Would you say that at that time the school was fulfilling its role as crucible of the Republic?

Above and beyond all our differences, we had a common religion. This was the religion of our studies, which we all shared—a common religion that united my communist family and my teachers, who were often Catholic and sometimes of the right. This factor was essential.

I will not get into the debate on the development of education in our country, but, without wishing to depict this era as a golden age, the fact that citizens, who were otherwise separated by political or religious opinions, were unified on one point, that is, not only the importance of education, but even, for the most part, the content of education—this was certainly a powerful factor of cohesion and even social friendship. French, Latin, Greek, mathematics—these were the heart of education, the four dragons that had to be conquered. The energy devoted to this task was enormous. You cannot imagine the care devoted to teaching us Latin and Greek—as much as was devoted to teaching them Nietzsche at the *college* of Pforta! Of course I am biased, but there was something precious that is all but lost today. It is very hard to know what holds a society together. We have many fewer political and ideological divisions, but other bonds that once brought us together have now disappeared, for example, the bond of the school, of studies, this bond by which we come to agree on what is important, on what it is important to learn in order to grow up.

Do you think this bond has been broken more by changes in the curriculum, or by changes in pedagogy?

I couldn't say. What would I say was the value of the education provided by the classic *lycée*? It was the extraordinary attention, the care given by the teachers of all disciplines to speaking an excellent form of French. The French language was the bond that held together all the subjects. We had a mathematics professor whom we feared and adored, as is often the case, and his mathematics classes were always French classes. He showed us that if we wanted to present a proof well, we must use this article and not that article, we must put a comma here and not there. Similarly, the history class was presented with perfect diction and drafted with extreme care. I am not saying that all the teachers were necessarily excellent, that all had an equally rich and profound teaching, but they all used great care to teach us the French language, the natural language that made it possible to say everything one could desire to say. This was true even in mathematics, even in history. The various disciplines were unified, in a way, in their extreme concern for the rigor of French.

This is not the place to propose a diagnosis of contemporary education, but I believe that what has done the most harm to teaching at the secondary level is the disappearance of this bonding role of French and the stance of independence of all the disciplines that want to speak their own languages. The mathematics teachers want to speak the language of mathematics, the history teachers want to teach the language of the science of history, the physics professors want to speak the language of the science of physics, and the children or adolescents are confronted with a fragmentation that is impossible to master, a fragmentation not only of the subject matter, which is inevitable, but also, one could say, of the form. I believe that here we have made some very imprudent decisions, when we renounced the centrality of the French language in education.

I. Apprenticeships

Does your interest in philosophy, however ambivalent it may be, come from the qualities of this classical education? Do you remember its origin?

That is hard to say. Between the ages of seven and seventeen, I was interested in political and scientific ideas. This is obviously linked to the communist sources of my education since communism presented itself as scientific and expressed a great confidence in science. And then there was my admiration for the Soviet Union and its exploits in the conquest of space, which led to an interest in scientific questions. And so I read books of popular science. Science was the ruling authority among us, the authority that was promoted by the authors that I read in the *Social Editions*. I remember particularly a book by George Cogniot, *Religion and Science*—the title tells you what you need to know of the content of the book.

At bottom, until my last year at the *lycée*, I did not know what direction to take between the sciences and the humanities. This last year was decisive. I chose to emphasize science and I discovered very simply that philosophy interested me more. This happened in a section of math students; we had a very good Kantian teacher, who was heckled horribly by the students, but who dealt with it very well. We had only three hours of philosophy, and the ritual never changed: at the beginning, he tried to speak above the tumult—all kinds of barnyard animal cries—then when the tumult subsided, my classmates started to divide up into groups to play cards just to get through the hour, and our professor came over to the little area where those few of us had gathered who were interested in what he was saying. Thus, he gave us private instruction within a class of students who had other things on their minds. In any case, this teacher, whose name, I think, was Monsieur Olivier, managed in three hours a week to persuade me that philosophy interested me more than anything. At the end of the year, I did not hesitate, but enrolled in the *hypokhagne* (preparatory class for advanced studies) provided by the same *lycée*.

So your first inclination toward philosophy was independent of your political interests?

Now that would be hard for me to answer, precisely because, at the age of seventeen, I was nowhere politically. I had begun to doubt communism, but I did not know how to leave it behind, and I began to take an interest in philosophy proper, as distinct from the sciences. But all that left me in great ignorance and uncertainty. One must also keep in mind the intellectual excitement that comes with the feeling of a certain capacity, at least as this capacity is evaluated by teachers. We move toward what interests us, and at the same time, toward what allows us to make use of certain powers that one feels one has. So that is it. That's the best I can do in reconstituting my state of mind in my last year at the *lycée*, precisely because I did not then know what I thought.

You also discovered Christianity during these years. Was this first encounter linked to the discovery of philosophy?

Encounters are always personal. I encountered communism because I encountered my father, one could say, and I encountered Christianity because I encountered my teacher in the preparatory classes, Louis Jugnet. He was a figure in the *lycée* of Toulouse where he had taught for many years. He was both a remarkable teacher and a singular and certainly a very endearing man. He was a Thomist; he belonged to the movement known as neo-Thomism. whose great figures in France were Jacques Maritain and Étienne Gilson. He led me to discover the immense domain of the Catholic religion, and of religion in general—but especially of Catholicism.

The first thing he taught me is that there is much to be known on the subject of religion. I did not know this before Jugnet, and I think many of our contemporaries are unaware of it today. For them, religion is, above all, a subjective feeling, or, in today's current language, a value. In any case, religion understood as having content that can be learned, that can be known, this was an idea that had not crossed my mind. And so whereas I had thought that to know was to know science, I discovered that there were many other things to be known, and among them was theology.

Jugnet greatly stimulated my desire to know because, even though his Catholicism was certainly very traditional and intransigent, at the same time, he emphasized the intellectual dimension of religion. I would say that, in his presentation, religion appeared as the dramatic deployment on a large screen of the problems that philosophy had brought to light. Religion appeared as a grand unfolding of the questions of philosophy that took these questions to their limits: essence and existence, act and potentiality, cause and effect, and all such questions. There was thus a cumulative effect for me in this simultaneous discovery of philosophy and of religion. I believe this responds to your question. My approach to religion was through speculative theology, and not through piety. This was a key factor in the path I took.

Was theology taught in philosophy classes?

No, you must not imagine that Louis Jugnet taught catechism in these preparatory classes at the *lycée*. What was specifically theological in his teaching he only shared with those who were interested outside of class. He answered our questions with extraordinary dedication! If you asked him two or three questions, a few days later you would receive a very clear and very detailed answer that filled six or eight manuscript pages. In class, the common class, he taught Descartes and Kant plus Saint Thomas. To be sure, he had no great sympathy for either Descartes or Kant, and one of his favorite targets was this formula that he attributed to Ferdinand Alquié: "Descartes and Kant are criticized only by those do not understand them." This sentence regularly incited sarcasm from Louis Jugnet. But in the end, it was philosophy and not religion that he taught us. One might say that he had no love for the Republic but did not depart from a secular approach. And in this classical and perfectly republican *lycée*, the teaching of this intransigent Thomist fit into the makeup of the establishment without any problem.

Jugnet had been a passionate follower of the nationalist Catholic Charles Maurras, and in fact, he retained an admiration for the nationalist Catholic that he did not expect us to share. Consider how strange this is: here is a man, Jugnet, who in his person combined all traits that today would cause him to be rejected immediately: a traditional Catholic and follower of Maurras, yet he was at the same time an incomparable teacher and one of the men most worthy of esteem that I have known. Moreover, the ultimate benefit I attribute to him is that he advised me to go meet Aron as soon as I was in Paris, that is, at the *École Normale Superieure*. I tell you, this was quite a man.

This question may be indiscrete: did not your interest in religion and then your political evolution cause tensions with your father?

I would not say tension. As much as this may surprise you, even though, when I was about twenty, there we were, he still a passionate communist and I in the process of becoming a passionate anticommunist, the affection we had for each other was not diminished in the slightest. This is not to say that we did not have some spirited discussions! My father certainly deserves the credit for this, because he suffered most from our disagreement. I was, and he is, at once extraordinarily passionate and capable of overcoming his passion and remaining just.

Did your mother participate in these discussions?

Once the discussion between my father and me had taken off, it was difficult to get a word in! In any case, my mother certainly was divided. Once someone asked her how she situated herself between her husband and her son. This is how she answered: when I hear my husband, I think he is right; when I hear my son, I also think he is right. I would say this is a judicious, and even an elegant answer.

THE 1968 YEARS

When you were at the École Normale Superieure, *did you feel this wonderment of which Aron speaks in his Mémoires?*

No, there was no wonderment at ENS. I was in awe of Paris, yes, but that's something else, but not the rue d'Ulm [location of ENS]. I was reminded rather of this verse of Baudelaire's: ". . . a sad hospital full of murmurings." This was rather my impression.

I wanted to be fair to the ENS—it is difficult. My fellow students, at least those who were politically active (which was a very large number), were divided up into various groups, in proportions that I could not determine: Maoists, Polpotists, humanist Stalinists and scientific Stalinists, Trotskyites of one or another observance, supporters of the Communist Party, etc. I did not know what I thought politically. I had taken leave of communism without yet having sketched an alternative doctrine or even orientation. In this milieu of the ENS, I felt as if I were in a ship of fools sailing very far from the real world—and it was this real world that I wanted to know and to understand.

When I speak of Polpotists and Stalinists, do not misunderstand, this was not the red terror. I was under no threat and I was free to criticize the dominant opinion. But there was no longer any common life at school; the politicization of the school had destroyed all life. It was no longer truly a school. Indeed, we used to raise the question: what is a school? For some, it was more like a hotel, for others a hospital, and for a significant number, more like an asylum. At least, those were the words that we used.

The result of this loss of a common life at school was that the great teachers that we might have desired to hear, such as Eric Weil for example, categorically refused to, offer courses. There were, of course, those we called the "Caymans" who were residents at the school. There was Jacques Derrida. Derrida welcomed me with charm, I must say, but I was immediately allergic to his rhetoric. Another Cayman was Louis Althusser. I have fond memories of Althusser. He was benevolent, even encouraging, judicious, but as you know, illness kept him for the most part far away from school.

I do not have good memories of the Sorbonne—since the ENS did not offer degrees, we took classes and received degrees from the Sorbonne. The quality of the professors is not in question; there were excellent professors. It is just that I had had enough of writing theses. I had once excelled in this method and now I was becoming simply mediocre. More generally, it was the kind of philosophy that was being taught that I found unsatisfying. The thesis machine was in the service of what I'm tempted to call industrial philosophy. The thesis machine and industrial philosophy—that really sums up the impression I had. The two great industries were Descartes and the Cartesian on the one hand, and Kant and German idealism on the other. These were the two great industries, the two great sites where we did our business, that is, where we were expected to do business. These were the authors: Descartes, Kant, Malebranche, Spinoza, Hegel, and Fichte; but, in my view, they were not so much interpreted as continually taken apart and put back together again, as one would a carburetor.

I risk being unfair here, but my sincerity is part of the contract interested in our conversation. I must say that I never sensed that any capacity for intelligence was really called for in this process of taking apart systems and putting them back together again. We were, for example, under the prestige of the immense work of Martial Gheroult; he was certainly a fine man, but one in whom there is not a sentence to be found that makes you think.

In short, I had fulfilled my hopes, since, starting from the preparatory class in Toulouse, I had made it straight into the ENS. But I spent these three or four years at the ENS drifting and very unsatisfied. I did not see the point of the required exercises and I did not know where I should turn. I even considered doing something completely different from studying philosophy. This dissatisfaction and this drifting could only come to an end when I would find the means, or when someone would give me the means, finally to access what seemed to me to be the things themselves, that is to say—and this will not surprise you—the political things. For, throughout this whole period, I was truly passionate regarding political questions, but I could not find a way to articulate them in connection with my philosophical studies. It was only when I would take part in Aron's seminar that I would find a way to unite my intellectual project and my political interests.

You speak of industrial philosophy, these great systems with their allegedly profound abstractions . . . it seems you do not think highly of modern philosophy—as opposed to the ancient philosophy whose merits you praise.

If I were asked to compare ancient and modern philosophy, I would give a clear edge to ancient philosophy, as you have noted. We will have more to say about this no doubt. But there is nothing systematic in this for me. There is at least one modern philosopher to whom my criticisms do not apply and who shares, in many respects, the merits of the ancient philosophers, that is, Rousseau. In any case, he is the modern author who has most interested me and whom I have most admired in a sustained way from the beginning. Now Rousseau must certainly be considered to hold a place in the canon of philosophers, surely even the canon of great philosophers, even if Kant or Hegel are generally considered more profound. But set aside profundity. There is no author who says more in fewer words than Rousseau, and there is no author who goes through all the facets of the phenomenon that he is determined to describe more rapidly or completely or with more finesse. There is no author capable of understanding with more impartiality the most varied or remote dispositions of the human soul. In every page of Rousseau, an infallible rhetoric gives expression to the most delicate and varied movements of the soul.

It may be because I am so impatient that I find his rapidity especially marvelous. Rousseau has already gone through every room in the house, from the ground floor to the attic, and is gathering plants in the garden while Kant is still asking whether and on what conditions he might be allowed to cross the threshold. But Holderlin said it well: with all his rapidity, Rousseau is "a soul of great patience." In the discourse on inequality, his winged pen tells the longest and slowest and most improbable story, that of the human animal becoming human. There is no denser text, ancient or modern. Of course, his popularity has damaged his glory, but he cannot be blamed for what fools have done with his words.

Rousseau was not included in the curriculum of the Sorbonne?

I don't recall taking a course on Rousseau, but he was certainly taught. Still, his place was very modest, and he did not contribute to the general spirit of philosophic teaching at the Sorbonne as I have tried to characterize it. There is, moreover, an interesting connection to make here: the more the academic philosophy became mechanical, technical, and systematic, the more political passions fermented, became focused, and heated up beneath the surface. They exploded in 1968. There, again, we observe a significant correspondence between the decline of philosophy and a disordered politicization of life.

These "1968 years" were a decisive time for your whole generation, politically and intellectually. Did you not have the feeling of being passed by?

Who passed by whom? I could say, like Châteaubriand, that my age missed its rendezvous with me. Of course, I am joking. But passed by? Perhaps . . .

How do I see things? During the 1968 years—we can give them this name—there were two great forces. I have just spoken of the first: academic philosophy, the great taking-apart of systems. And then there was the other body of thought, which has become known precisely as "the thought of 1968"—the thought that considered itself subversive in relation to academic philosophy. This thought was very varied. There was, of course, the triad of suspicion—Marx, Nietzsche, Freud—and then there were structural anthropology, linguistics, psychoanalysis.

To answer your question, if in retrospect I compare myself with the majority of my fellow students or members of my generation, I realize that I was simply indifferent to most of the thought of 1968. I cannot say I was hostile, because hostility presupposes a certain familiarity; I was indifferent. I was a close friend of Nicolas Ruwet, a great linguist, but I could never really read what he was writing. I was indifferent to linguistics and to psychoanalysis. Obviously, I never joined any political, ideological, or editorial group linked to this thought.

I am sharing with you this observation without offering any interpretation. If I wanted to think well of myself, I might say that a sure instinct caused me to avoid foods that my metabolism could not assimilate, and that I judiciously saved my strength. "Why get into Lacan, psychoanalysis, or linguistics? You will get nothing out of it." Maybe that is what my instinct was telling me. One could also say that I was precociously hard of hearing and incapable of hearing the intoxicating music of the spirit of the times. Choose whichever interpretation you prefer, or another that might suit you.

In any case—and I know that when I say this, I must provoke at least incredulity—the "1960s" has never been important for me; "1968" was not a moment in my development. Too bad for me, one might think, but so it is. I cannot even say that I learned not to follow the trend; I cannot even say that I experienced my own independence, because I did not even realize how indifferent I was. It was only in retrospect, much later, that I told myself: "all that went past you like water over a duck's back!"

Still, I would not want to suggest that I was living in an airtight compartment. Some of the references of the period concerned me greatly: Marx and Nietzsche, of course. On this point, I shared the interest of my fellow students: Marx and Nietzsche, and also, along with Nietzsche, Heidegger. I imagine we will speak further of these authors. In those days, I was bewitched by these authors, along with everyone else.

What other authors or kinds of works attracted you, if not the canonical works of the period?

Through this whole period of the ENS, I really read without any rationale or plan. Why, for example, did I read the complete works of Charles-Albert Cingria, a very appealing Swiss author of whom I have forgotten everything? Following the inspiration of the moment, I drew from the well-furnished and very accessible library of the Rue d'Ulm, an excellent library with excellent librarians to whom I am very grateful.

In any case, it was on the shelves of this library, already in my first or second year, that I found Hannah Arendt's *The Origins of Totalitarianism*, which I read in English—it wasn't yet translated in French. Later, I was severe enough with Hannah Arendt to be able to say now that this was certainly one of the books that made the biggest impression on me during my years at the ENS. Now it is clear to me what I might hold against her, but still, there was something in this book I had been seeking up to that point in vain, that is, a powerful way of articulating the century's political experience in connection with some analytical concepts, with some criteria that would make it possible to impose some order on the century's experience. This is certainly one of the books that kept my spirits up in a period when I lacked confidence in my own strength.

In this reflection on totalitarianism, do you think you were looking (even if the intention was vague) for a solution to a personal problem—the temptation of communism and a way out—or were you looking for a solution to the intellectual impasses of the age?

Your question is very pertinent. For me, in effect, the years marked by 1968 were dominated by this question: how intellectually to get out of communism? I had left the communist side without knowing in what direction to launch. I was not alone. At least since the Hungarian revolution of 1956, this had been an urgent and even a piercing question, especially in our country, and it was still an important question for many in France in the years of which we are speaking.

I. Apprenticeships

There was a tendency, a temptation to which it was easy to succumb, that consisted in essentially renouncing politics, and saying that real life is elsewhere—a slogan that was supposed to deliver us from slogans. Communist ideology politicizes everything so much that it is tempting to be free of it by this renunciation, or it is tempting, once one is free of it, to renounce political reflection.

Here is an example. In those days, there were works inspired by Marxism that were not without value. I am thinking particularly of works by Lucien Goldmann on Racine and Pascal, or, to a lesser degree, of Pierre Barbéris on Balzac. The natural reaction of those who were not Marxists or who were not taken up in Communist ideology was to say: what is wrong with these works is that they politicize the subject, that they introduce politics where it does not belong. This was a tempting reaction, but I believe it was a bad reaction. The good reaction would have been to discern the right view of politics that would possibly have made it better to understand Balzac or Racine or Pascal. Thus, the first thing to avoid, I would say, in leaving communism behind, was to leave politics behind. What was important was to understand that the problem with communism was not that it is political, but that its politics are not really good.

At the same time, or inversely, the power of communist ideology—its hold on people—consisted in its grasp of the political aspect of things; this grasp was, to be sure, very unilateral and narrow, but it was strong. Thus, in a sense, for this reason its prestige and attraction were, I would not say justified, but understandable. For communism was confronted most often only by political objections, or rather, by denunciations of the political reading of intellectual works. This was, as I have said, a very bad answer. The point, therefore, where the repudiation of communism is concerned, is not to renounce the political perspective, but to broaden it and refine it. To leave behind the ideological politicization of thought by elaborating a political philosophy is, it seems to me, what my generation has tried to do. With how much success is debatable, but the direction is incontestable.

This project was all the more necessary because, as I have already mentioned, there had no longer been for a long time a political philosophy in France that presented itself as such. The expression itself was practically no longer claimed, with the exception, I believe, of Raymond Polin.

This showed in the way authors were approached, to return for a moment to this topic. In a class on Hegel, for example, the political part was always subordinated: the Encyclopedia, the system, the logic, that was worthy of the best minds. But the German constitution, or even the principles of the philosophy of right, these were really for the foot soldiers, those who did other things, those who were not up to the level of the system.

How do you explain this disappearance of political philosophy in France?

There was no longer any political philosophy, especially in France, because, among other reasons, what we now call "political philosophy" did not have its own place within the university. It was caught between a rock and a hard place, as the Americans say. On the one hand, as I have said, there were the philosophy departments where it was regarded as a poor sister or a vulgar relation that one took in out of the goodness of one's heart in a shack beside the impressive edifice reserved for "pure" philosophy. On the other hand, it was methodically driven from departments and institutes of political science, precisely because what defined departments of political science was their rejection of political philosophy as "nonscientific" in order to replace it with what seemed to them to be true science, that is, of course, "political science."

Thus, there was no place for political philosophy, and it was very badly treated. Here is an anecdote that is not pleasant to tell, but that captures the disdain in which the best minds held it in the 1960s and 1970s. One of my philosophy professors at the Sorbonne, who liked me and whom I liked very much, when he learned that I was determined no longer to work with him but that I was turning toward political philosophy, offered this philosophic commentary: "Yes, of course, political philosophy, you can live off of that."

Well then, to conclude on the subject, I would not say, like the generation of the *dreyfusards*: "we were great men, we were very great . . .", but still, I would say that our generation, we who have tried precisely to elaborate this political philosophy, we deserve some credit for bringing sleeping beauty back to life.

PART TWO:
PHILOSOPHY, POLITICS, AND RELIGION

RAYMOND ARON AND LEO STRAUSS

On the advice of your preparatory class teacher, you met Raymond Aron. How did the special relationship you had with him begin?

First of all, I probably would have gone to see Aron even if Jugnet hadn't recommended I do it. Still, it pleases me that there was a kind of—let us not say apostolic succession—but a kind of passing down of the witness, as in a relay. Each person who has played an important role in my intellectual life has passed on the witness to one who would be responsible for my education in the next phase. In this, I find a reassuring sense of continuity and coherence.

I described the state of mind I was in before meeting Aron, the perplexity in which I found myself before the task of elaborating an intellectual project suited to my interest in political things. I wanted to return to the things themselves, to use a familiar formula. For me, the return to the things themselves, or the beginnings of a move toward political philosophy, is closely tied to my relationship with Aron. Here again, the personal factor is decisive.

It is difficult to speak of such a relationship. I would have to say that there is an element of passion and love. I was carried away with admiration for Aron when I met him. And the Friday seminar, in the old building on the rue de Tournon, immediately became the most important thing for me. There was no question of missing it for any reason to the point that I sometimes forgot the most obvious professional duties. I am not proud of this but it is time to admit it. I was teaching in *lycée*, and when there was a staff meeting scheduled at the same time as the Aron seminar, even if I was supposed to take the lead, there was no way I was going to the meeting; obviously, I would go to the Aron seminar. In retrospect, I tell myself that I should've gone to the meeting, that there would have been another seminar the next week. But at that time, there was no question of missing any part of the Aron seminar.

This gives you an idea of the state of my mind and heart. I must add, because relations between student and teacher can involve all kinds of motivations, that no one was less interested than Aron in personal influence or in dominating a young man. Nothing in his conduct suggested the slightest desire for or pleasure in such influence; he had no interest in captivating an auditorium or an individual, unlike others in his generation who were virtuosos in this art. Aron was not at all like that. Of course he was concerned that his work be recognized and that his political analyses contribute to forming the public mind, but he had no interest in power over souls. By instinct, by nature, as much as by conviction, he knew how to live only in freedom, his own and that of others.

In any case, I believe I can say that we formed a very warm friendship, despite the many years that separated us.

Did you already admire his books or was it his teaching that captivated you?

Before teaching me through his books, Aron educated me first of all, and I would say especially, by his very person, that is, by his way of holding himself in the world and of practicing his humanity in the world. By his very being he made it clear that only a long education of the intellect and of the faculty of judgment makes it possible to find one's way with some certainty in political life. In this way, he delivered us from the contempt or disdain for politics that comes so naturally to intellectuals, even or especially to those who are "politicized." By the way that he gathered and synthesized the information he needed for all the subjects he treated, he demonstrated that, in politics too, there is something to be known.

I would have liked to avoid this well-worn comparison, but there is no doubt that, whatever one thinks more generally of his work, what distinguishes Sartre's political judgment is that it is perfectly incompetent, if the adverb is compatible with the adjective. Sartre never knew what he was talking about concerning politics.

Aron, whatever one thinks of him more generally, knew what he was talking about, and by this very fact he educated his reader or his listener because he showed that there was something to be known, and therefore that political judgment, far from being derived simply from our values or our choices, from our "project," is based on the patient analysis of the political things themselves.

Of course, Aron wrote a lot, but I would say that he was first of all a talker. Moreover, his writings—this is at once their strength and their weakness—were fundamentally spoken texts. Aron did not write, if you distinguish between writing and transcribing his own words. When Aron wrote, he did not do the work of a writer; hunched over his writing pad, words came to him naturally. He wrote as he would have spoken. This is what gave his writings their direct, strong, and trenchant character, and also what detracts a bit, obviously, from their quality as a written work. His books are projections of his speech, and so they are not quite the finished works that one would sometimes wish.

Aron was above all a speaker, and I have the sense, shared by many who knew him, that his speech possessed an authority, and a simple eloquence that belonged to him alone. On this point, I recommend the text that evokes, better than any I know, Aron's speech. This is the article by Alain Besançon entitled "Raymond Aron à l'oral," which was published in the volume of *Commentaire* honoring Aron after his death. Its invocation of Aron's speech is extraordinarily suggestive and very true.

Aron allows us to appreciate the natural authority that speech can have. In the text that I drafted in his honor when, at the end of his life, he received the Erasmus prize, I tried to understand Aron's role under the category of the orator in the Roman or Ciceronian sense of the term, that is to say, a man in the public square, who speaks with authority and competence and eloquence on public affairs. This, for me, was Aron's greatness. This is a rare greatness; in my view, it is a human type that is more rare than great scientific competence for example, and that is most often underestimated. Consider Cicero's reputation, the unhappy Cicero: for how many centuries has he been treated with condescension?

Aron had followed a long intellectual path before becoming what he was. He has told his story in his *Mémoires*. Aron only becomes Aron in the years just before the war, when the stakes of European conflicts—in particular, of course, the rise of Nazi power—cause him to find his way and his voice. Daniel Mahoney notes that the first remarks in which Aron makes his voice heard, in which he is entirely himself, is his speech before the French philosophy society on the eve of the war, in which he denounces pacifism. He had thus followed a long path: he had left [France to study in Germany] a very good student, an excellent student, a perfect student in the French academic tradition, a highly estimable tradition but one that is quite deficient where political things are concerned. And although the early Aron, I would say, the Aron before Aron, held some interest for me, still, I was not urgently interested, neither in the commentator on German sociology, nor even in the author of the *Introduction to the Philosophy of History*, even if I have carefully read this book, which was based on his thesis. Thus, to repeat, it was Aron the orator who definitively or decisively captivated me.

You also discovered Leo Strauss in this period. How is it that, captivated as you were by Aron, you took such a passionate interest in this Platonist?

Aron turned me definitively toward political things as the site where human life finds its proper tension and reveals its stakes. At the same time—and here I am obliged to bring to light the imbalance of my intellectual situation at that time—as impressed as I was by Aron's approach to politics, I was looking for a reference point beyond politics. Perhaps my interest in theology played a role in this, but, in any case, even within the philosophical domain, I felt the need for a criterion of politics, a reference beyond politics that might supply a criterion of politics.

Aron understood my preoccupation, but such questions had no urgency for him. He spoke commonly of "regulative ideas": "Yes, of course, we need regulative ideas, in Kant's sense, to orient us in the political world," but actually he got along fine without them. He made perfectly attentive readers who were not much interested in politics believe he was a Kantian. But Aron was the least Kantian thinker there is; he sought no horizon beyond politics, no "kingdom of ends," no "pure morality." He inhabited the immanence of human things without anxiety; for him these things obviously contained their own rules: what must regulate human things is apparent in the very immanence of political life. There is no need to go looking above or elsewhere, as long as we assume— and he never considered another hypothesis—that human beings are not entirely depraved. If men are normally constituted, the rules of human life emerge in the very exercise of their humanity. I would say that Aron was the perfect gentleman who experienced no need of transcendence. The immanent rule of humanity sufficed him. Maybe, after all, he is right. Maybe that is wisdom. But for my part, I impatiently desired some "measure," to speak Plato's language, some transcendent measure, or at least some measure that allows a synoptic view of life and thus would make it possible to regulate life. There you have it. And this impatient desire for a measure, Aron could not satisfy it because he did not feel it himself.

Aron understood immediately that I wanted to follow a path on which he could not guide me. He suggested that I read Leo Strauss, believing that I would find in Strauss something that would answer this need, that I would find in Strauss the Platonist something that would bring me closer to my goal. I've always been grateful for this and I continue to admire Aron for it, since I believe it takes a very generous soul to point a young man with whom one has entered into a relation of friendship and confidence, toward an author, a colleague in a way, who one knows will take precedence with this young man. Aron led me to Strauss knowing that to go toward Strauss was to distance myself from him. He did it very spontaneously and naturally. This generosity confirms that Aron had no desire for power over minds. He gave each person what seemed to him best for that person without worrying about his own influence.

Aron's influence was, therefore, doubly decisive for me: in teaching me how to approach political things and in leading me to Strauss.

How did Strauss's influence prove decisive, as he took over from Aron?

Strauss did not take over in the sense that I left Aron behind. As a reader of Strauss, I continue to be attentive to everything Aron wrote, said, and did. Still, it is true that, where purely speculative thought is concerned, Leo Strauss has had the greatest influence on me. He is the author with whom I have debated most intensely. To explain myself in this connection, it would be necessary to trace broadly how I see Strauss's work. I shall try.

Strauss rediscovered the Ancients. What does it mean to "rediscover the Ancients"? This means, first, that he discovered an alternative to the Moderns because he had good reason to doubt the wisdom of the Moderns. The axis of Western higher education aims, or tends, to make us spectators in the triumphal march of modern philosophy since Descartes or Bacon. We applaud the great procession and we applaud our own applause. This triumphal march of modern philosophy leads up to the crowning moment, the symphonic orchestra, the great systems: Hegel and German Idealism. In the face of this great orchestra of modern philosophy, we hear Strauss's discordant voice, at first almost inaudible—a very sober and reticent voice. It is like hearing, I am tempted to say, beside the crescendo of this symphonic orchestra, the austere and virile monody of a Dorian flute. But this music of Strauss's is such that, once it has got into your system, you are profoundly taken by it. All the forms of prestige under which we live are subverted to the point that we find ourselves asking this radical question: does this huge deployment of modern political philosophy, with the huge institutional machinery that we have built in large part according to plans laid down by this philosophy—do these not finally have the effect of separating us from nature, and in the first instance from our own nature? In short, Strauss raises a question mark over everything that seemed victorious, over all the solutions we have taken for granted, over all the conclusions that seemed beyond doubt. This is just what happens: radical doubt insinuates itself in all areas of knowledge and thought. We find ourselves obliged to ask the question: what if the modern project is carrying us ever further from ourselves? What if this moment when humanity thinks it has finally succeeded in possessing itself is, in fact, the moment when it is the most distant from itself?

Were you not predisposed to hear this discordant anti-modern music?

To be sure. A certain sensitivity to the pathologies of modern democratic society, a certain anti-modern sensibility, if you will—no doubt we will speak further of this—opened my mind to Strauss who is, of course, not just any anti-modern; it is Strauss who sought most vigorously and most rigorously to find the root of the modern project and to bring it to light as a political project. Thus, in the face of this official history, in the face of this "progress of the Enlightenment," in these works that are like no others, these works that one does not know how to approach, Strauss brings to light an alternative history in which the modern project is no longer the superhuman realization of reason but an altogether human project, a deliberate political project that begins with Machiavelli and by which Europe commits itself to the huge enterprise of "acquiring the world" in order to achieve the mastery of the human condition—a mastery that may coincide with the greatest alienation or loss of self. This is one of the first aspects of Strauss that captivated me.

Strauss is also famous for his rediscovery of the "ancient art of writing." You know what this means: he rediscovered what was, according to him, common knowledge up until the 18th century, that is, that before the founding of modern politics, philosophers were never candid in public; they did not think it desirable or possible that the philosopher say publicly "what he really thought." By publishing candidly his thoughts, the philosopher would put in danger first of all the city, whose laws and opinions he criticized, and then himself, since the city would punish his effrontery, as happened to Socrates. Therefore the philosophers had to make use of a certain art of writing—an "esoteric" writing—in order to communicate what they wanted to say.

This idea horrifies and scandalizes our contemporaries. They feel personally betrayed: "What, you are saying that Plato, who says such beautiful things, is lying to me?" And the idea that a philosopher could lie to them—*to them*—this is something they cannot accept. They do not ask themselves whether the philosopher does not do the right thing by avoiding the danger to the city of too much candor. Still less do they ask themselves whether the philosopher does not give sufficient indications of his true thought to those willing to make the effort.

And for your part, what pleases you in this philosopher's lie? Is it political prudence? An approach of necessary condescension toward the city?

You are mistaken. This reader of whom I have just spoken, who cannot bring himself to believe that Plato is lying when he says such beautiful things, I am this reader! I started as a modern reader myself. Only gradually did I appreciate the liberating significance of Strauss's discovery. To say very briefly what would require hundreds of words, Strauss's analysis of the ancient art of writing liberates us from the "sociological point of view" that tends to determine the way we look at our humanity. This point of view presupposes that in the works of the mind we simply find the signs produced by society. The works of the mind absorb and render the signs produced by society as a sponge dipped in water absorbs and renders this water.

What Strauss shows is that works of the mind, especially those of philosophers, are governed by the philosopher, and that the social signs that one sees in a work of the mind are those the philosophers conveys to society, not those that he necessarily receives from it. For example, if a philosopher lives in a society pervaded by religion, he will use religious language, first of all, simply to make himself heard. The sociological perspective that we have absorbed leads us to say: There are religious signs in this philosophical work—Hobbes speaks of God and of Jesus Christ; Locke speaks of God's law—therefore, these authors share the religious views of their society, since the opinions that shape the human mind are always those of "society." But Strauss shows, in a very convincing way, I think, through the extremely careful study of certain fundamental works of political philosophy (Machiavelli, Hobbes, Locke), to what extent their religious references are part of a language mastered by the philosopher. Far from showing that such authors are subject to the pressure of society or that they are expressing their adherence to socially dominant opinions, he shows that they are using words that are familiar in the society in which they express themselves, in order to say things to this society, or at least *in* this society that it does not want to hear, things that go well beyond what it is ready to accept.

So did you read Machiavelli, Hobbes, and Locke with the Straussian decoder?

There is no Straussian decoder. But it is true that there are certain "tricks" you need to know to look for in this "art of writing." Some "tricks" are common to all philosophers, like their way of beginning and ending an argument with conventional views, and placing subversive views in the dense middle of a text. And then there are tricks proper to each author. The Straussian reader takes a childish, and therefore very serious, pleasure in seeking them out; it is a kind of treasure hunt. I noticed, for example, while reading Locke's *Essay Concerning Human Understanding,* that the author accompanied his most audacious propositions with a casual "but this by the by."

That said, what was most important for me in this area was not the art of writing as such. As I suggested above, what matters most—and here I don't want to be bombastic, but to say things clearly—is the mind's freedom. Strauss's rediscovery of the art of writing is a demonstration of the mind's [*esprit*] freedom. That sounds like a slogan: who could be against intellectual freedom? We are all for intellectual freedom, but we all (or almost all) think that the mind is determined by society. So tell me what intellectual freedom is if the mind is determined by society! Strauss shows that at least some minds can liberate themselves completely from society's pressure in order freely to go about their work, being capable at once of taking account of the interests and prejudices of society and of making known to the reader who is sufficiently attentive to the text what he really wants to say that is far removed from the prejudices of society. In this sense, Strauss is indeed a great liberator.

Strauss's demonstration has very important implications, particularly for our understanding of the place of religion in so-called Christian societies. Why is this? According to the sociological point of view that I have tried to characterize a little bluntly, the prejudice of the philosophy of the Enlightenment, the prejudice of our public philosophy of history, is that there were ages of faith in which everyone, so to speak, was a believer, and that now we have left behind the age of faith and every individual believes, or more often does not believe, according to his choice. They had no choice and now we have the choice! This idea plays a decisive role in the received interpretation of European history, to which we will no doubt return. But Strauss shows that certain authors of the so-called age of faith, who seemed to be good Christians, or at least passable Christians, and who, in any case, called themselves Christians, in fact, if one reads them well, showed themselves to be rigorous critics of Christianity and sometimes implacable atheists. In other words, the obligation to believe characterized the public space but minds were still free. And the most vigorous among them found ways to share their doubts with their readers. In brief, the sociological point of view, and this history which is determined by it, transforms the domain of commandment and of political obedience into a social necessity, a kind of "anthropological" necessity. When the political regime requires public recognition of the truth of Christianity or of a given Christian confession, and when the members of society comply more or less eagerly, there is, indeed, "social pressure" that motivates every individual to say what must be said and to do what must be done, or to pretend. But the social pressure derives ultimately from political government. Ultimately, I might say, the members of society obey the Prince more than they are "caused by society." The mind is free, in effect, and even if the free mind can be made to obey, to go along, and can forget its freedom, there is no way that it can be "caused by society."

Strauss thus helped me to loosen the hold of the "social-historic" point of view and to reconsider European history. I came to see secularization theories more and more as sociological fables based, I repeat, on the postulate that there are ages of faith in which man was necessarily religious, that there were forms of society in which human beings were necessarily religious. Secularization theories subject the human mind to necessity—and it is again by necessity that the human mind liberates itself from the necessity of religion. Let me say this as plainly as possible: if there were many atheists during the age of faith, and if there are still some believers in the air out of secularization, then our whole theological-political history must be reconsidered.

You say that Strauss is the author with whom you have debated most intensely. What does that mean?

Yes, Strauss nourished my torment over many long years. He nourished it particularly for the following reason. As I said before, I had discovered philosophy and religion together. I had discovered them from a Thomist point of view, within the serenity of the great Thomist edifice in which, in a way that is obviously very satisfying, reason's conclusions come together harmoniously with faith's propositions, or at least prepare them. Strauss, on the contrary, emphasizes that philosophy and religion are two incompatible ways of life, and that one must, therefore, choose: either/or. I had entered into this question of philosophy and religion through a Thomist portal, and now the man with the greatest power over my thinking explains to me that Saint Thomas was certainly a great thinker who elaborated an impressive synthesis between philosophy and religion, but that in such a synthesis one risks losing what is most essential in each of the elements because, in reality, the way of philosophy and the way of religion are two self-sufficient ways that cannot be joined. One cannot commit oneself at the same time to the philosophic way and to the religious way, to a way that is necessarily one of "skeptical" inquiry and to a way that presupposes the truth of revelation—law or sacred scripture. For a long time, I wandered and hesitated between the equilibrium and the beautiful architecture of Thomism and Strauss's austere demand that I choose between philosophy and religion. So where am I now? I'm still looking.

Did you not already consider the Thomist tradition defective as it relates to politics?

No doubt the Thomist school is strange; on the one hand, we owe much to them. The Thomists have preserved Aristotle, they have studied texts, they have continued the analysis of virtues, of prudence and justice, the analysis of action, of deliberation and of rational choice. . . . We are in their debt for much. On the other hand, their Aristotle is an Aristotle almost completely detached from his political context and his political concerns; their Aristotle sometimes has little to do with the real Aristotle. In the 20th century, even when they deal with politics, the Thomists often use the least political parts of Aristotle's *Politics*, for example, the reflections of Book One on natural communities, and in particular, on the family. The Aristotle that the Thomist tradition deploys is usually one who is merely preparing his political analysis proper. Thus, there are whole stretches of the politics that are ignored. Consequently, the Thomist approach to the virtues tends to neglect the political context of their exercise, to dilute them into simple "moral virtues." While I recognize that so general a diagnosis is necessarily simplified and unfair, I would say that the Thomists have moralized and depoliticized Aristotle. It is strange, but also very touching, in a way, to see that the deepest thinker or the most complete analyst of the democratic city has been preserved as canonical in moral and political thought by interpreters who were often "monarchists"; In effect, the neo-Thomist school was long dominated, at least in France, by authors who were political followers of Charles Maurras. The history of neo-Thomism thus provides a fine example of a noble intellectual tradition that fails to establish an authentic link with actual political experience. Consider for example Jacques Maritain, an eminent mind and a remarkable man in many respects, but one who went from being a follower of Maurras to a democrat without changing his Thomism. This is because, fundamentally, doctrine was independent of political experience and analysis. It was a metaphysical and moral doctrine—on being, intelligence, will—that made full use of Aristotle but that was not really interested in political experience, even though this experience was at the heart of Aristotle's work.

One might say that, generally speaking, the Thomist tradition is weak where politics is concerned. On this point, in the debate between Strauss and the Thomists, Strauss has a clear advantage. If I now feel distant from the neo-Thomist school within which I received much of my philosophical education, this is because this school has been shaped by its lack of any living connection with political experience; it looks at political experience "from above."

Strauss asked you to choose between religion and philosophy, but did he not help form your judgment on political things?

Strauss rarely gave his views on political events, but each time he did, he provided texts that I find remarkable in their political wisdom and political judgment. I am thinking in particular of a text on "German nihilism," written during the war, that is notable for its breadth of vision, its rigor and its equally admirable sobriety. Strauss rediscovered and allowed us better to understand, above all, the Greek or Aristotelian approach to politics, which is, I would say, the political approach to politics. It is truly he who, for the first time in a long history, reformulated what should be the way of political philosophy, or of political science as originally understood. He emphasized that the point of view of political science or of political philosophy is not radically distinct from the point of view of the citizen, that it is, instead, its extension or refinement.

Our political science presupposes, on the contrary, that the scientist or theoretician must by no means believe a word spoken by citizens. He is the one who knows. He is, scientifically, the subject and they are the object. Notice the *tone* of much contemporary political science: the reader must be impressed that the author is an Expert, that what he says is based on Science, and that such an expert has nothing in common with the unfortunate citizens that one observes as if they were insects.

Strauss reminds us that political science must arise from the citizen's perspective because political life is founded, in the first instance, on the idea citizens conceive of it, that is, on the idea, or rather the different, sometimes opposed ideas of justice that they form. Political science in its full and original sense is simply the most rigorous possible treatment of the question of justice as this question is deployed naturally in political life.

Leo Strauss intended to rediscover the original and, according to him, authentic idea of philosophy. It seems a very radical idea. Do you adhere to his description of philosophy?

No. This is a point that separates me from my American Straussian friends. I have never really succeeded in making sense of this "philosopher." As much as his idea of the way of philosophy, the "dialectical" way interests me, his idea of philosophy remains foreign to me, for there is a point or a moment in his presentation, and perhaps even more in that of certain of his students, in which philosophy leaves this earth, where the philosopher separates himself almost entirely from the human being, and at this point, I can no longer follow Strauss or even see where he is going. . . . To be sure, science as such has a necessarily "inhuman" dimension, insofar as it is "disinterested" and thus presupposes the suppression or at least the suspension of ordinary human interests. One must, to a certain degree, separate the scientist or the philosopher from the man. But I have never been able to understand the figure Strauss sketches of a philosopher who would fulfill his being by completely abandoning all interest in human things, who would leave all human interests behind. I find more humanity in religion, in the religious person, than in the philosopher as I conceive him, or rather as I cannot manage to conceive him, a philosopher above all human things, for whom justice becomes a secondary consideration and for whom human bonds are of no real interest.

How is it possible to hold together a philosophic way that rehabilitates political experience as the source of science and an image of philosophy totally detached from human things?

Your question is very pertinent. You put your finger on what seems to be a contradiction. I have emphasized that Strauss's political science was an engaged science, because it extends and refines the engaged, and often even passionate, point of view of the citizen. At the end of his investigation, the thinker does not arise at a viewpoint that is disinterested but at one that is impartial. One must be very interested in the question of justice to desire to be impartial! Otherwise, one is only indifferent. At the same time, it is true that the thinker as thinker does not share the condition of the citizen. The citizen may know something of the aspiration to a certain impartiality, but he tends to be partial and partisan. Political life is moved by "parties." The thinker, for his part, seeks instead what is just in the point of view of each party. This rigorous impartiality contains something that is, in a way, superhuman or inhuman. It is this disposition that contemporary political science wrongly interprets as a point of view radically distinct from that of the citizen— a purely "theoretical" point of view. Tocqueville said this very well and very simply: for true political science, the point is "to see not otherwise but further than the parties."

I have not yet answered your question, which concerned, as well and first of all, the philosopher. According to Strauss, philosophy is not limited to political philosophy or political science, which remains turned toward human things. But man is not all there is, he is not The Whole. There are, therefore, "higher things" than man. Let us take an example. Political life is governed by a law of alternation between movement and rest. After the movement of war comes the rest of peace. This is a matter of political science. But movement and rest as principles are higher and more vast than the movement and rest of human beings. The philosopher, as distinct from the political philosopher, is concerned with principles of movement and rest, and thus to this degree, he is no longer concerned with the movement and rest of human beings; he turns away from human things. Up to this point I understand, and I do not see any contradiction in Strauss's views. What perplexes me is that, according to Strauss (or so it seems to me), the philosopher is defined in his being by this point of view, and thus he represents an entirely distinct human type, a type having the characteristic of being "more than man." There you have it. I've done my best.

How did you come to know Strauss's work? Is there one of his books that particularly influenced you?

My first exposure to Strauss's work was through *Natural Right and History*, which Aron had recommended to me. Strauss's writings are notoriously difficult to access. Thus, his original influence was not so much by his writings, but rather by his oral teaching. The Straussian school (and it really is a school) emerged in the classroom. Moreover, this school is not really comfortable outside the classroom, while it is at its best in the classroom. This is because it is a school that attaches great importance to teaching, and thus to oral teaching, since, in a sense, there is no teaching but oral teaching.

I was fortunate to meet one of the most remarkable and surprising members of this school, Allan Bloom, who was very close as a student to Strauss and whose whole life was devoted to oral teaching. And it is through Bloom that I had access to the oral tradition, which helped me read the books that were also available.

Now, since I have mentioned Bloom, we must talk about him.

I would like to say that, in order to speak of Bloom, one would have to be a writer, but apparently that is insufficient, since Saul Bellow wrote a book about Bloom that did no justice to the subject matter. This book is called *Ravelstein*, and it has, incidentally, been translated into French. No doubt I will do no better than Bellow, but in any case one could not do worse. Still, I would like to give you an idea of the person who helped me understand the meaning of the American expression "larger than life."

He was quite a stylish man, with an elegance that was perhaps a bit garish; his physical presence conveyed authority, and he was full of wit and wry humor. He was passionate for what the Greeks called "fine and expensive things." (This is a point on which Saul Bellow emphasizes a little too readily). One of his most striking traits was his interest in and affection for children; he took an extraordinary interest in children, even the very small ones. And his affection was, moreover, much appreciated.

If I were to attempt to summarize what made Bloom charming, in the strongest sense of that term, I would say that he possessed two attributes that seem incompatible. On the one hand, there was his overwhelming experience of an encounter with a master of philosophy, an encounter that had set the course of his life from the first time he had heard him at the age of 17 at the University of Chicago. From this moment, he never aspired to anything more than to understand better what Strauss had taught him. There was thus, on the one hand, the overwhelming experience of a master teacher of philosophy. On the other hand, there was the inextinguishable self-confidence of an American in the American Century. And the conjunction in his person of what I would call these two opposite orientations—this highly improbable conjunction elicited a powerful sense of wonder, in the primary sense of that term. There was at once the humble disciple of a wise man whom no one knew and the Lord of the new world dominated by America. The way he mixed these two orientations of his being gave him a charm that was all his own, at least in my eyes. But I was not the only one so affected, because I remember that, in our little group, when we told each other around the month of May or June, "Bloom is coming!." the mood was joyous because he brought with him a contagious joy. This improbable visitor brought new scope and energy to the life of Paris, which had become so predictable for us, but which he loved so much.

This was something very important to note and something that distinguished him: he loved Paris and he loved France intensely and profoundly. What I am telling you is not anecdotal. You might say to me: "Fine, he loved Paris, he loved France. Many others also loved Paris and loved France; that is not enough to make someone interesting." This is true, but I believe that today, at least according to my experience, there are simply no longer any Americans who take a real and sincere interest in Europe and in a country of Europe in the way that Bloom was interested in France and loved France. I believe this is one of the major parameters of the new situation of the West: the Americans, whatever they may say, no longer feel any real and sincere interest in the countries of Europe. They are no longer interested in Europe, or in France, or in Germany, or in Italy, or in England, as a human whole from which one might learn something important. I believe that there has not been an American for twenty years who felt the way Bloom felt. Bloom loved and understood the French difference, what is distinctive about it, the spirit of the nation. He was capable of tasting all its complications, and all their finesse, with an attitude that I would say was pure generosity, not as something picturesque, but as representing the fulfillment of human possibilities such as could be found in America. For Bloom there were in France ways of life, types of human beings, and experiences that were not possible in America, and thus he was grateful, in a way, to France for providing him the opportunity to encounter these experiences and these human types, these ways of life. Perhaps today these human types, these experiences and these ways of life are disappearing. In any case, the French difference or the spirit of the nation, setting aside wines and fine dining, no longer holds any interest for Americans. On the contrary, the French difference appears to them in a grimacing expression from which they have nothing to learn and in which, besides, they find nothing lovely.

I noted with sadness this change in attitudes of Americans concerning our country in the person of certain of Bloom's students, whose acquaintance I made as they accompanied him to Paris, and who progressively took a more and more negative view of France. In this sense, and of course this goes well beyond his person and my experience, Bloom is paradigmatic of what was a moment of equilibrium, a period of equilibrium in the Western world, I would say, between America and France: this is when a victorious and triumphant America was still capable of recognizing a certain spiritual dependency in relation to Europe. Of course, the Americans knew that they were stronger, that they were richer, and that the new century belonged to them, but they were still capable of recognizing that there were certain things in the European experience that perhaps came from a more distant source, and perhaps went beyond the American experience.

Today, this possibility is lost, either because Americans have lost the curiosity and generosity of Allan Bloom and others like him, or because we have lost what made us attractive and worthy of such interest. I do not know which explanation is better; perhaps a mixture of the two, but it is certain that the relationship between the United States and Europe is much less interesting today, if it is even still possible to talk about a real relationship. There is simply a country that goes on with its life, the United States of America, and then there are the European onlookers.

How, in your view, do Europeans regard the United States?

It seems to me that it is hard for Europeans to form a balanced judgment of the United States. And by balanced I do not mean cool or indifferent. I believe that anyone who aspires to understand modern politics must gain some understanding of the United States, and to do this, one must have some love for the United States. I do not mean to make love for the United States obligatory, but I think a minimum of sympathy and of recognition of American accomplishments is a basic prerequisite for a minimal understanding of politics, both contemporary and more generally. To take a narrow, negative, and contracted view of American life and of the action of the United States since its founding is not only an injustice toward the greatest political success of the modern world but also signals a missing element in the comprehension of political things—a missing prerequisite for an impartial approach to political phenomena in general. This is because, despite all the criticisms that one can and must level at America, the United States remains a truly unique and powerful political phenomenon.

For my part, let me say, perhaps with a little solemnity, that it is thanks to Bloom that America became part of my life. Many of his friends and students became my friends. And finally, it was with Bloom's help, although after his death, that I went to teach for some time in the United States.

You have described Bloom as a person. What distinguished him as a philosopher?

As I've said, Bloom was mainly a teacher. He became "rich and famous" because one of his books was extraordinarily successful, but producing books was not what he was about. He produced books by accident; this was not the essence of his life. The essence of his life was in teaching, in the classroom, in the small class and the small group in which, without bothering to shave, one discusses the interpretation of a text of Machiavelli or Plato. He was an admirable commentator on authors, on philosophers, in particular Plato and Rousseau. His commentaries on Plato's *Republic* and on Rousseau's *Émile* are evidence of this.

The book that made him famous, *The Closing of the American Mind*, arose out of a particular circumstance. Bloom had written an article on the spiritual and intellectual situation of American universities that Bellow found striking. Bellow suggested he make a book of it, and he did. In this book that was thus made to order, he set forth a diagnosis drawn from his teaching experience with energy, passion, and a kind of violence: the education dispensed by the universities had impoverished the souls of students. Note that the language is Platonic. And so is the underlying thought: education concerns the soul, which it perfects or causes to deteriorate. Thus, in his eyes, higher education in the United States generally tended to diminish the souls of students, in the name, in particular, of the new virtue of "openness," which, in our societies, sums up or rather replaces all the intellectual and moral virtues. He showed quite convincingly—and this is not, by the way, specific to America—that openness so understood promotes relativism and finally, indifference to truth of any kind. One of the arguments that provoked the most hostile and perplexed reactions was that in which Bloom, ever the Platonist, described the effects of rock music on young people as follows: a barbarian ecstasy that renders the soul incapable of all education of feelings and tastes.

To what degree did [Allan Bloom] shed light on Strauss for you?

Bloom helped me realize how radical a thinker Strauss was, and how troubling in the strong sense of that term. This is because I have attempted to interpret Strauss as he presents himself in *Natural Right and History*, that is, as a conservative friend of freedom, with a particular understanding of the rupture brought about by modern political philosophy, and thus, as a thinker who allows us to continue to conduct our lives, if I may say, with respect for natural affections. I remember saying to Bloom, who was speaking of the philosopher as I was describing him a moment ago, as one who leaves behind him all human affections and human interests: "Still, Socrates loved Athens . . ." We were at the café *Le Rouquet*, on the Boulevard Saint-Germain. He looked at me in a way that meant: shall I really tell him the truth? Can he handle the truth? He must have thought I was capable of handling the truth because he said to me: "No, Socrates did not love Athens, he did not love his wife, he did not love his children . . ." and the unspoken conclusion was clear to me: "There, if you want to be a philosopher, this is the perspective you must take seriously."

I have always been struck by how much Strauss's students are in love with Socrates. Socrates is their permanent or final reference, and the figure of admiration *par excellence*. Maybe Strauss discovered the true Socrates, which, of course, cannot be reduced to what Bloom told me on the occasion I have just reported. He certainly helped to make him interesting for me, but not to make him attractive or loveable. I could even say this: nothing is more troubling or "perplexing," nothing is more worth thinking about than Strauss's work on the figure of Socrates. And yet, at the same time and in a certain sense, in my eyes Strauss made of him an almost repulsive figure.

So Bloom told you as a philosopher in a friendly way that the philosopher has no friend?

Not exactly. Bloom loved his friends; he did not love the family. He tended to oppose these two kinds of relationship. There is no doubt that he loved his friends very much. In fact, this was an objection that I sometimes made to him. He showed much interest in them and paid them much attention.

One day, when he must've been arguing once more for philosophical indifference, I said something like this to him: "So why are you so interested in talking to my daughters, who are between three and eight years old, and with whom you cannot have philosophical conversations, even if you have fun together?" His answer was something like this: ultimately, the philosopher is only interested in philosophy, but to be interested in philosophy is to be interested in a soul capable of philosophy, and to be interested in a soul capable of philosophy is to seek a soul capable of philosophy. Thus, the philosopher is naturally interested by other human beings because he cannot help himself. He is looking in their souls for signs of philosophic arrows, for interest in philosophy. It follows, necessarily, that one with a philosophical temperament must take a particular interest in other human beings." This was a strong answer but it did not entirely resolve for me the question raised by the strange inhumanity of the philosopher: what is he looking to when he turns away from human things?

That said, Greek philosophy demonstrates an incomparable psychological discernment, and if the Greek philosophers tended to leave the human sphere, they certainly derived an extraordinary capacity to understand the movements of the human soul from this adoption of a distant standpoint. Ultimately, the reason why Plato, Aristotle, and the Greeks in general represent an incomparable source of education is that they possess this understanding of human motives that I believe we have in part lost. From this point of view, Bloom did much to rectify my original inclination, as a good student in the French tradition, for general ideas, and to help me see philosophy otherwise, that is, not as a way of elaborating ideas, but as a certain human possibility. Man, or at least a certain type of man, is capable of distancing himself from the urgent interests of human life, of suspending these interests in order to raise questions to which he will not find certain answers, and ultimately of suspending and, as it were, dismissing the fear of death in order to reflect on the articulations of being. In other words, every person is taken up in the necessities of the interests of life, but the philosopher discovers that there is some play in the soul, play from which most human beings are not capable of benefiting, from which only those with philosophical natures can benefit and are thus capable of this distancing. Here is an example: the central part of the human soul, the part that, as Strauss said, renders human beings "interesting," is what the Greek philosophers called *thumos*. This might be translated "heart" as in "Rodrigue, have you any heart?" This is the faculty by which one defends oneself and one attacks, one fights for justice and one is sometimes driven to injustice. Now Strauss said that the philosopher as such has no *thumos*. So is this human type who so interests us deprived of this very part of the soul that makes human beings interesting! I will thus say a little flatly: philosophers would not have been able to discern and distinguish the role of *thumos* in human life if their souls had remained prey to *thumos*, if they had not entirely overcome it.

In any case, Bloom helped me focus my attention on the fact that the most interesting questions of human life play out in the realm of motives: what are the motives of human beings? It follows that philosophy is finally self-knowledge since, obviously, one cannot really know human motives without being capable of knowing one's own motives. Self-knowledge, in effect, is not the knowledge of the *self*, of the "I", the knowledge of one's individual, incommunicable or incomparable particularity; this self-knowledge consists in discerning how human motives, the motives *common* to all human beings, are configured in one's own soul. If I am indignant at the injustice of another, it is perhaps because it touches on my own injustice. As I denounce it, I fail to understand it. I can only understand what is unjust about it if my own disposition is finally just.

Thus, philosophy culminates in, or at least results in, self-knowledge. This is what the Greeks call "putting one's soul in order." This is something that seems at once noble and hollow when set in this way—"the wise man puts his soul in order"—but Bloom, following Strauss, made it concrete and relevant for me. Bloom brought me to understand Strauss's proposition that the result of philosophizing, the liberation brought about by philosophy, is simply the ordering of the soul. Thus, philosophy in its original meaning entirely escapes the artifice of systematic, conceptual constructions and finally consists in finding the right disposition in which to hold oneself in the world, or in relation to the world.

I return now to what I was saying in the beginning, in opposing Strauss's Dorian flute to the great orchestras of modernity. Philosophy, from Strauss's point of view, presents itself as extremely modest, discreet; but at the same time it possesses a hardness—I won't say of diamond, because a diamond is something dead, but rather that it has an unequaled strength of penetration and resistance. It is the summit, the extreme limits of the strength of the soul. And this idea of philosophy continues powerfully to interest me, even if this extreme limit escapes me, even if I do not find this strength in myself.

Do you not recognize yourself, after all, in this definition of the wise man who has discovered the freedom of his own soul and who knows how to distance himself as necessary in order to analyze human motives?

I have tried to be as clear and, at the same time, as honest as possible in laying out my perplexity. I am not very impressed, as you will have noticed, by the portrait of the superhuman philosopher as drawn by the Straussian school. *I don't buy it* [English in the original]. But the understanding of the soul as elaborated in the Socratic tradition seems to me to be the most convincing and dazzling part of the "science of man" that is possible for us to know. This above all is what I have learned. I have tried to make good use of this in my effort to understand political things. So, to respond to your suggestion, no, I would really have trouble appropriating a description of wisdom concerning which I feel such perplexity and reticence. But I would claim a certain competence in political things, and this is a competence acquired along an educational path for which the study of Greek political philosophy has been and remains central.

RELIGION AND HUMAN EXPERIENCE

Recapitulating the various influences that have marked you, I note that there are three poles: the political, the religious and the philosophic. How, finally, do you hold these together?

I am inside a triangle: politics, philosophy, religion. I have never been able to settle on one of the poles. Aron situated himself within the political, Strauss the philosophic, and Maritain, let's say, the religious. Of course, I can say that the world draws upon these three great sources, that it turns on these great axes and therefore that, in keeping my distance in relation to these three points, I remain open to the diversity or complexity of the world. This is a flattering answer, but frankly it is not satisfying. The reason is that politics, religion, and philosophy represent three human attitudes, each of which requires complete devotion. Churchill cannot be a philosopher or a religious man if he wants to be Churchill: he is too busy with "human things." Strauss and Socrates cannot be statesmen or men of faith: if they turn away from human affairs, it is not to attend to the Father's, but in order to pursue an endless questioning. Likewise, a religious man cannot be a philosopher in the full sense: he can employ philosophic tools very competently, as Thomas did with those developed by Aristotle, but he has already given his soul to the Answer that precedes all questions, or rather he has answered the Call that precedes all questions. He might conceivably become a statesman, but how passionately will he defend his people when his heart is turned entirely toward God?

There are thus three human attitudes, each of which claims a complete devotion that I cannot or will not grant to any of them because the two others also appeal to me. I find a fragile equilibrium, or rather a productive disequilibrium, in this questioning that I pursue concerning the very manner in which these three dimensions are articulated throughout Western history. I have the idea, or the illusion, that, by taking each of the three equally seriously, I attain a certain impartiality in understanding this history.

And yet one either believes in religion or one doesn't!

Of course. But it is already very hard to know oneself in general, and one's relation to religion is perhaps the most difficult thing in the world to sort out. I'm going to try to tell you a few things, but I will not succeed in overcoming my essential timidity on this subject. Doubtless words will fail me.

My disposition was marked from the beginning by a certain ambivalence or, rather, by an inner division. The more I came close to religion, the more I entered into it, the more on the other hand I had contact with the effects of religion that did not win me over, or that, in some respects, put me off. Even while Catholicism, in its doctrinal architecture, seemed to me to represent the crystal of every desired truth, I took note of its political incompetence and its effects in this domain that I would describe without hesitation as corrupting. Just as I was being received into the Church, most of my reading was devoted to Machiavelli, Hobbes, and Rousseau, that is, to the most ferocious and convincing analysts of this incompetence and of the corruption of politics by the Christian religion. And since the political order is the heart of the human world, this "Machiavellian" doubt concerning religion's political effects tends to spread to its effects on the human world in general. As much as I admire the Catholic tradition of spiritual discernment—in truth, there are a number of schools in this tradition—piety as such left me rather cold and mistrustful. I would put it this way: piety leads us to expect a holiness from which one is, in general, naturally quite distant. Thus the pious and sincere man – I'm not talking about Tartuffe, who is a completely different case—cannot help acting as if he experienced feelings that he does not experience, as if he had thoughts of which he cannot in fact conceive, and even as if he saw things he does not see.

This difficulty is no one's fault, but it gives the life marked by religion, governed or inspired by religion, a character that cannot completely sustain my conviction. Péguy spoke very well of such things, of the way in which the religious perspective and the simply human perspective have trouble meeting. You remember his brilliant formula in speaking of the teacher and the priest: "The one who holds the confession does not have the trust." I would say that this formula sums up, for me, the problem of the place of religion, at least that of the Christian religion, in human life.

Let us stay with Péguy a moment. You know his commentary on *Polyeucte*. This is one of his great pieces! What interests Péguy in *Polyeucte* is that it is one of the rare works of a Christian author—for Corneille is Christian—that preserves the integrity of the human realm. This is to say that the Christian author does not pull down the world in order to elevate religion. The human realm in *Polyeucte* is constituted by human love and human honor in the trio formed by Polyeucte, Pauline, and Severus. What Péguy emphasizes is that Polyeucte is not satisfied with having the truth for himself, the Christian truth. (He has just converted to Christianity.) He wants to be the equal of Severus, the Roman knight; he wants to be his equal and perhaps to surpass him in exercising human virtues, those of human honor and human generosity. Polyeucte is capable of meeting Severus on the level of paganism, the level of human virtues, of human honor.

In short, Péguy's concern is the same one honored by Corneille's Polyeucte: not to pull down the world in order to elevate religion. This is what distinguishes him, as he rightly notes, from a certain tendency in Pascal. A formula in his commentary on *Polyeucte* sums up his thought—and I end with this citation, which is as brutal as one might wish or fear: "The error of the devout party is to believe that they are people of grace because they lack the strength to be of nature."

In a more general sense, does the theological apparatus that you admire seem to you faithfully to describe human experience?

I am inclined to say with Pascal that the Christian religion "has well understood mankind." The problem lies in the way in which this science is formulated when it is a question of guiding human beings. The Catholic teaching is framed in the name of the "natural law," and it proposes under this rubric many things worthy of our interest and attention and that bear, as far as I can tell, at least an important part of the truth. That said, one of the most characteristic trials of human experience lies in the fact that law and nature are rarely in agreement. Thus, in order to establish a doctrine on the natural law, it is still necessary, if I can put it this way, to prepare the material. In order for human nature to appear receptive to religious law, or at least capable of receiving it, it is sometimes necessary to pretend not to see things it is impossible to ignore. We are then necessarily obliged—and I have no better solution—to make all sorts of little accommodations with the truth as we experience it, accommodations that are often inevitable but that, taken all together, finally draw a portrait of human life that is not notable for its verisimilitude. This is one of the major difficulties, to repeat, of the relation between religion and life. I do not blame religion for its ambition to change life and to perfect human beings, to make them "perfect as their Father in heaven is perfect"; that is its *raison d'être*. But where the articulation of the religious experience with human experience is concerned, we have to admit that religious people sometimes lack certain scruples where experiential truth is concerned when they propose an understanding of humanity already pre-treated for the uses they have in mind. In such cases, the Answer has smothered the questions.

A work that satisfactorily brings together fidelity to human experience and commitment to a religious perspective is rare. Or, rather, in my opinion, there is only one work, one text in which the two are strangely, paradoxically reconciled. No surprise here: this work is the Bible, especially the Old Testament, in which we find at once, directly and immediately, human experience in its greatest ignorance of God and, mysteriously, a presence of God that does not impinge upon, that does not cover up, the authenticity of experience. The text of *Psalms* is particularly overwhelming because, in a chaotic and popular language, it maintains a balance that the greatest religious minds have not been able to maintain so perfectly. This is a text in which we find a human being who complains, who cries out in pain, who protests, who wants to kill his enemies, who is afraid of dying, who is sick, and, mysteriously, at the same time, we find an experience of something radically different from all human experience but which does not prevent this experience from being lived and described in its whole truth, in its nakedness. This, in a way, is an argument for the "revealed character" of the Bible, in that it includes texts that manage to hold together what no human being can hold together within the limits of human expression.

Let me add one thing. Why, finally, would the Greeks not be enough for us? They understood everything that was essential to understand of human things, and they said it with incomparable sobriety and force. And yet there is an accent that is neither in Homer, nor in Plato, nor in Sophocles, namely, precisely what denotes this inconceivable proximity between human fragility and divine holiness: "My bones were not hidden from you when I was made in secret, skillfully wrought [embroidered] in the depths of the earth." [Psalms 139:15. King James: "My substance was not hid from thee, when I was made in secret, *and* curiously wrought in the lowest parts of the earth."]

Since you often insist on the importance of personal encounters, have you not known Catholics who measured up to your idea of a religion faithful to the truth of human experience?

I did not particularly wish to have ties in Catholic circles. Besides, more generally, I was never preoccupied with joining any circle. Still, necessarily, I have met Catholics. When I arrived in Paris, I met certain people who were to be very important for me: Stanislas and Aniouta Fumet. They were very old, and I very young, and this distance alone produced a charming effect. In their presence, I came in touch with a world, let us say a world prior to the University, a world in which literary life was at the heart of national life, where artistic and intellectual life were inseparable, and also where Catholicism was still ambitious and domineering.

Stanislas was a writer, journalist, and editor, and he lived amid poetry, music, and mysticism. He spoke to me of Maritain's circle, and of Claudel's, of this France still stirred by great passions, and thus of great thoughts and great works. He was a small bearded man, merry, jocular, and colorfully dressed.

But it was especially Aniouta, his wife, who was surprising. She was a lovely elderly lady, dressed in white—it seems to me she was always dressed in white—who brought you immediately into a world truly very different from the one you had left at the door. It was all about the play of grace and of freedom. God was perpetually and visibly active in Aniouta's world. She had a very immediate and very concrete feeling of the presence of the other world in this one, since angels and saints filled her most ordinary conversation. Her piety surprised me but did not put me off at all, quite the contrary. She could appear extremely naïve, but actually Aniouta was capable of the finest intellectual distinctions and of great spiritual discernment. She was highly educated and well-read; she had met many great minds, yet, at the same time, she saw your guardian angel very clearly over your shoulder, or she would point out to you, as naturally as can be, to what saint you should pray, urgently, if you had a problem with plumbing or financial worries.

To return to your question: Aniouta, in effect, possessed something that is rarely found among religious people, or people moved by religious passion, or by religious interest. She was perfectly natural; she covered the whole spectrum of religious life and of profane life as naturally as can be. This is what I found enchanting in this little salon on the *Rue Linne* where the Fumet couple received so many young people. They had countless godchildren, since they brought about conversions with impressive regularity and efficiency. They even founded an order of knighthood. What one did in this order I do not know, but I know I was a member. I even had a name in this order—obviously a secret name.

I realized, years after the deaths of Stanislas and Aniouta, that they had played a very great role in the life of many young Catholics, and not only Catholics for that matter. Truly, they represented a kind of personal, informal influence whose equivalent it is difficult to imagine today, since now everything is mediated by institutions, whether universities, colloquia, or Erasmus grants. . . . We can no longer imagine a salon that welcomes in people as they did over thirty, forty, fifty years, that educates, instructs, and charms all different kinds of people who share the experience of this salon. Yes, I have known a mystical dwelling where all was grace and freedom.

Did you meet some people in this mystical dwelling?

In fact, I was generally alone when I saw the Fumets, but I still met a few people there. I think particularly of someone who has, I feared, rapidly disappeared from the French scene, although he was a major voice for many years. I speak of André Frossard. You may know him; he had a humorous column in *Le Figaro* for about thirty years. Every day he published under the title "Lone Cavalier."

Frossard, like Fumet, had never attended the University. He was self-taught, and supremely intelligent. He spent his life flicking verbal darts while gesturing with his cigarette holder. I never saw him do anything else but take shots while smoking. His mind produced these darts as an apple tree produces apples; he could not help himself. I have never known anyone with such a quick wit. He was a very troubled, very secret, very complex man. He had had some awful private sorrows; he was very ironic and very dark. He liked me, but could not forgive my love for Rousseau. He could not manage to reconcile the favorable idea he had of me with my love for Rousseau, in whom he saw the height of immorality. He had been close to Raymond Aron, but their differences concerning de Gaulle had put distance between them.

One day he said to me: "You Aronians, you Tocquevilleans, you liberals, you are very intelligent, you combine institutions and constitutions, you separate powers, which is all very well. But I think simply like Aristotle: if in the city there is a man who in his virtue manifestly surpasses all others, we must without hesitation give him the power; it's the just thing to do. But you refuse to see that we have in our midst such a man, we have de Gaulle. He is in power, and I am happy. What else would we seek?" I was struck by the argument, and I still find it worthy of interest. But what is surprising is that Frossard, at the same time, judged de Gaulle severely for the spiritual risks he took in entering into a political career, a career that Frossard judged to be altogether hellish. Thus, Frossard was grateful to de Gaulle for saving the country, all the while blaming him for losing his soul, or at least putting it at risk.

I much appreciated his intellectual freedom, but, as you can see, he was of little help in resolving the theological-political problem.

FROM THE ARON SEMINAR TO THE JOURNAL *COMMENTAIRE*

If there is one place where you made important connections, this was Aron's seminar.

Indeed. The very special atmosphere of the seminar had much to do with Aron's personality (to which I shall not return), but also with that of the other participants. What was interesting for me as a young man was that most of them were already well along in their intellectual lives; they had already a work or the beginning of a work behind them, and they found themselves in Aron's seminar for reasons essentially analogous to my own—that is, they had found a refuge far from the ship of fools. In Aron's seminar, I thus met people who had their own interests, who were involved in a work or a project they could offer to me, and who had knowledge to transmit to me. This was a gathering of strong intellectual personalities who deferred to and admired Aron, yet still maintained their intellectual independence, even in relation to Aron.

It suffices to name Jean-Claude Casanova, Alain Besançon, and Jean Baechler, just to mention those who remain my closest friends. One indication of the freedom of our intellectual exchanges on a truly crucial subject of the times is this: throughout the whole duration of Aron's seminar, or at least during the time I was there, Besançon and Aron argued about the true nature of communism. Moreover, one could say that, at the conclusion of this debate, Aron moved closer to Besançon's position. This was therefore a gathering of independent minds, each having its own view of things.

A second feature of these intellectual personalities was that they were unclassifiable by academic discipline. Casanova was trained as an economist, but 1,000 things interested him more than economics, I think it is fair to say. His readings in literature, philosophy, history, and law are immense, and it would be ridiculous to call him an economist, despite his competence in economics. Besançon holds the highest degree in history and is a historian, but he is also a writer, theologian, and philosopher. Baechler is the author of an encyclopedic work that is unique today in the West— one must use terms that are almost solemn to speak of Baechler's work—even though, in fact, very few people in France are aware of the importance of this work.

It will appear that I am praising my friends, which is very bad form because this is well known to be a way of praising oneself.

But I think it is useful, not to do them justice, since they have no need of my kind words, but to draw attention to a more general phenomenon that is proper to France: namely, the existence of these intellectual figures not tied to any discipline. Indeed, my modest knowledge of intellectual life in different countries suggests to me that one thing that distinguishes France is that there are among us quite a number of individuals who have produced considerable work that cannot be classified according to the standard academic categories. These authors are interested in all things that are interesting, and they are capable of saying interesting things on every subject they take up. Obviously, they are exposed to the reproach of the scholarly bureaucracy that they are dilettantes, and so they represent a figure of intellectual life that is now threatened with extinction.

These friends that I have mentioned taught me a great deal, not only through their presentations in the seminar, and not only through their books, but also by the substance of their ordinary conversations. There was, in effect, in and around Aron's seminar, the kind of spontaneous conversation that is at once absolutely serious and absolutely full of laughter, in which one speaks of the great questions that interest us as political and rational animals without subjection to the rules of academic discourse. Besançon's conversation was like this, as was Casanova's and Baechler's. The result was that there was never, in our way of life, any distinction between the life of work and the life of leisure. In this sense, I found in Aron's seminar and the friends I met in the seminar a very convincing example of what the ancients called "life of leisure" or of *otium*, since this is the life that we led and that we are still trying to lead.

It was also in Aron's seminar that you first met Claude Lefort.

Indeed, it was in the seminar that I first made the acquaintance of Claude Lefort, who had just published his great book on Machiavelli. This would have been in 1972 or 1973. Aron suggested to me that I write a review for the *Archives Européennes de*

Sociologie, which I did. And this review provided the substance and the occasion for my first exchanges with Claude Lefort.

This man is warm and abrupt, ferociously independent and very respectful of the independence of others. We never became very close, but despite the generational distance, we formed a trusting friendship to which our political differences added some spice. Lefort has always encouraged me and, for my part, I have always been very interested in his work which is inspired by phenomenology and strives to recover a grasp of the political as a generating principle of the human world. How does democracy reconstitute the human world? In what way is it haunted by its opposite, totalitarianism? These questions have preoccupied me, and Lefort offered complex answers that gave me much to think about.

In 1970, one of the participants of the seminar, George Liebert, along with Patrick Devedjian, launched the journal Contrepoint. *To what degree was this an extension of the seminar?*

Liebert could tell you better than I, but it seems to me that *Contrepoint* was the meeting ground of the Aron seminar and of Liebert's personality. Liebert was indeed a participant in the seminar. He was quite young at the time, just coming out of *Sciences Po (Institut d'études politiques)*, and he already had a very strong personality. Liebert was, in a very striking way, a man of passion(s), in the singular and the plural. To refer again to the psychology of the Greeks we were discussing earlier, Liebert is first of all the man of *thumos*, that is, of this part of the soul that disposes one to defend his friends and to attack his enemies. And if democracy, as Tocqueville explained, tends to atrophy this part of the soul, then George Liebert is certainly the man most resistant to democracy I have known. In any case, he does not resemble the democratic man described by Tocqueville, and he has no intention of resembling him!

It was truly a joy to participate in this endeavor, led by a young man who was very ardent, very combative, very intelligent, and a very good editor. His passion did not prevent him from possessing very sure judgment in evaluating and correcting texts, or from knowing many things, for he was also a person of much knowledge, even erudition, and who had a taste for very precise citations and references. This combination of passion and great editorial competence, along with the variety of his interests—all this made Liebert a sort of maestro particularly capable of running a journal unlike any other. This journal was at once very free in its approach and very exacting in its form, its format, its references; it included very long texts—more extended essays than articles—and it evinced a pronounced taste for intellectual combat.

We were in a combative mood, but Liebert was the most combative of the group, and so it made sense that he was at the head of our little band. In this journal, Jean-Claude Casanova already played an important role, as did other participants who would later come together at *Commentaire*. I think *Contrepoint* was really the first crystallization of a movement and a friendship that still endures, albeit through all sorts of dramas and avatars and metamorphoses. *Contrepoint* really helped to lay the foundation for our history together.

On the subject of the combative spirit: you yourself write some articles in this period that manifested a certain thumos.

To be sure. Strauss, as I mentioned earlier, says that the philosopher has no *thumos*, and so I was absolutely not a philosopher by this definition. In retrospect, I am indeed struck by this combativeness. We were all combative. This was not simply a question of personal temperament; it was, in a way, a feature of the times, because today, the encephalogram may not be flat-lining, but *thumos* certainly is. For the last twenty years one has the impression that France is sedated. We were not sedated. And most of the articles of my youth, taking this term in an extended sense, were very combative articles—polemical or very polemical. I would not say that I regret this youthful tone, but certainly I now look at this fiery young man with a certain surprise.

This fiery attitude expressed itself notably in certain articles on René Girard. Did you find this author particularly meaningful?

Indeed, René Girard was an author who greatly interested and pre-occupied me.[1] I wrote two articles on him, one in *Countrepoint*, and one in *Commentaire*. This is an author who deserves a bit of our attention.

René Girard produced one of the most interesting bodies of work of the century, of the second half of the century in France. Or let us speak rather of works written in French, since, as you know, after studying at the School of Chartres, he went to the United States, where I believe he taught French literature. From the East Coast of the United States, he kept his eye on the French intellectual scene. This scene was dominated by the social sciences, which drew either upon structuralism, and especially upon the structural anthropology of Claude Lévi-Strauss, or upon psychoanalysis. Girard took an interest in all these grand theories of the 60s, but he said: "These theories are nonetheless insufficient; I have in mind a much better theory that can explain what they explain and what they cannot explain, a theory that explains these theories themselves."

Thus Girard, far away from France, and yet focused on Paris, elaborates the theory that will take account of other theories and succeed, in a way, in introducing the final theory, the ultimate explanation of human society and civilization. One might say that Girard brought about the "apocalypse" of the social sciences, in the sense of their "revelation."

This is not the place to expand Girard's thought, but let me present a few of its elements in order to explain my attitude toward him. For Girard, human civilization is based on the mechanism of the emissary victim: human beings, who are naturally subject to violence, to undifferentiated violence, are reconciled to one another through the death of the emissary victim. Undifferentiated violence

---

1   "René Girard, la violence et le sacré," *Contrepoint,* no. 14, 1974 ; « La leçon de ténèbres de René Girard, » *Commentaire*, no. 19, automne 1982.

comes to an end when the members of a society, or those who will be its members, put the emissary victim to death; civilization reconstitutes itself with its differentiated order on the basis of this putting to death of the victim. This is the violent origin, the violent root of all human civilization, according to Girard.

It is Christianity that puts an end to this violent routine of civilization, since, according to Girard, it delivers up the secret of the human world, the secret of human civilization, the secret ignored by all civilizations and all religions before Christianity: the victim is innocent, absolutely innocent. Henceforth, therefore, humanity is haunted by the Christian truth. And yet, apparently, since humanity remains what it is, it never manages completely to recognize this truth, even though it is haunted by it. This truth—one must not, moreover, say this Christian truth, but this truth of humanity revealed by Christianity—is the innocence of the victim, and it is the fact that the protagonists of violence, those who make war, are *the same*. The truth, in this sense, of the human condition, is this reciprocal violence in which we are all *the same*. And only Christianity, according to Girard, makes it possible for us to see this anthropological truth that, in all our wars, disputes, conflicts, and acts of violence, we are *the same*. René Girard's is a great and subtle mind, and these brief indications cannot, of course, do justice to his work. But this, in a few words, is the heart of his teaching.

I have always found this teaching powerful and impressive; and, at the same time, it has always seemed to me unacceptable and, in fact, particularly dangerous. For one of its consequences, naturally, or one of the presuppositions of this teaching, is that the human order has no internal consistency and no inherent legitimacy. In any case, political order loses all consistency and legitimacy, because, if the basic truth of civilization, of human society, is undifferentiated violence and that we are all the same, in which case there is no reason to distinguish among political societies or among political regimes, no reason to recognize that one regime is after all better than another, and that a certain cause is nevertheless more just, if only a little more just, than another cause. In this sense—if I may put it a little crudely—by this interpretation of

II. Philosophy, Politics, and Religion

Christianity as the ultimate revelation that we are all the same, and by propounding this anthropological truth, Girard encourages and radically justifies what seems to me to be the political vice of Christians, or the political vice encouraged by Christianity, that is, a potentially perverse preference for the enemy whom we have been commanded to love as we love ourselves. Or, to say it a little less crudely, Girard tends entirely to erase a line that is difficult to draw in this area, the line that separates holiness from indifference to justice, and which easily transforms itself into a preference for injustice.

Here I am using the term holiness in a broad sense; I am not a theologian and am inclined to accept correction from the magisterium that is responsible for the precise meaning of these terms. As Montaigne would say, here I am speaking as a layman. Understood broadly, holiness implies a certain detachment in relation to one's own cause, even a just and good cause; perversity implies a secret attachment to the enemy's cause, even if it is bad. In Girard there is a certain systematic incapacity—an incapacity rooted in his system—to understand political situations, because political situations are always to some degree conflictual, and Girard always returns to the same fundamental truth that, in a war, the only truth of war is violence, and the only truth of violence is its undifferentiated character, and that, once again, the two protagonists are ultimately the same. All political situations come down to the same fundamental situation, which, moreover, is not at all a political situation because it consists in violence without a trace of justice.

Obviously, in a situation in which equality is posited between the enemy and ourselves, there is a tendency to prefer the enemy. This is what I call the perverse tendency of a certain kind of Christianity where politics is concerned. It hastily and imprudently transforms the Christian proposition according to which we are all, in a sense, equally sinners into a political proposition destructive of all political morality: ultimately, among human causes, there is no difference in justice, no difference in honor. Péguy would surely fulminate against Girard, who strips human virtues, in particular courage, honor, and justice, of all meaning, in the name of a supposedly more profound anthropological truth.

In 1978, barely two years after the end of Contrepoint, *the journal* Commentaire *appears. Its president is Raymond Aron, and you are one of its co-founders, along with Jean-Claude Casanova, Marc Fumaroli, and Alain Besançon among others. How and why was this new collective enterprise born?*

Commentaire was born because *Contrepoint* went away, for reasons it would not be useful to go into here. In any case, *Contrepoint*, founded by Liebert, had come to an end. And so it was necessary to find its successor. But, apart from this, it seems to me that *Commentaire* was born in different circumstances than those that attended the birth of *Contrepoint*. *Contrepoint* was born in the context of Liebert's jubilant anger. *Commentaire* was born under the pressure of another passion, an eminently political passion as well, that is, fear. I emphasize this because this fear now seems incomprehensible and almost ridiculous.

What fear am I talking about? This was a fear, externally, of the progress of communism and a fear of the Union of the Left in France. Obviously, when you explain this today, you are met by indulgent smiles: "What, you were afraid of communism, of the Union of the Left? And you call yourselves historians and political analysts? But you have missed the whole point of the story!" In fact, we were afraid, and I believe we had good reasons, or plausible reasons to be afraid.

Let us put ourselves back in the context of the end of the 1970s: the Union of the Left, the alliance between socialists and communists is solid, or at least it seems to be, on a basis, it must be said, that grants much to the communist point of view. Meanwhile, in the rest of the world, it seems like the communist movement is taking full advantage of its assets. We must remember—and here I will recall events a little later than 1978, but which convey a sense of the period—that, in December 1979 Afghanistan is invaded, and that in 1980 Sadat is assassinated; this is the time when Cuban troops transported by Soviet planes conduct the brilliant Carlota Operation in Angola. One really has the feeling that the communists are on the offensive and that the United States and the West are in a defensive position. Carter is humiliated by Khomeini, and Europe is dominated by a pacifism that proclaims "better red than dead!" Germany is flirting with neutrality. In a word, it was neither paranoid nor pusillanimous to think that the situation was not favorable to freedom.

There was an additional factor, closer to us, and that is that we worried that the left, once in power, would be unfavorable to the newspaper in which Aron wrote, namely *Le Figaro*. So it was also a matter of assuring that Aron had a platform. Thus, we hastily conceived the idea of constructing a frail vessel on which freedom could still be defended. You may smile, but this was, in fact, the way we saw things.

And so we met in the office of Alain Besançon on the rue de Bourgogne. We had considered all kinds of titles. I proposed *The West Wind* to counter President Mao's East Wind, but my suggestion was declined. We chose *Commentaire* after a long discussion: *Commentaire(s)* in the plural or the singular? Finally, we found that *Commentaire* in the singular was much more noble. This obviously does not prevent most of those writing the name of the journal, when they want to speak well of it, from putting *Commentaire* in the plural. This we had foreseen.

You conceived Commentaire *as a platform for Aron. In the end, did he play a central role in the journal?*

Aron was central to *Commentaire*'s founding, as it was an extension of his seminar and of his deeds, but it must be added immediately that *Commentaire* was and remains fundamentally the work of Jean-Claude Casanova, because it was he who has been its director and indefatigable moving force from the beginning. *Commentaire* is the reflection of Jean-Claude's personality, of the variety of his interests and his talents, of his political orientations and his literary sensibility. Of course, since his is a catholic soul, in the etymological sense of the term, he has always left plenty of space to others, including those whose political sensibility was quite different from his. In the end, in any case, *Commentaire* is Casanova's work.

Would you say that Commentaire *was rather an intellectual than a political journal? What made it distinctive in relation to other journals?*

As I have said, the first concern of the journal was political, that is, to give a platform to liberals in a very broad sense. And at that time, to be a liberal was to be an anticommunist liberal, for in the enterprise of *Commentaire,* as before in *Contrepoint,* there was a solid anticommunism in a country in which communists found not only many supporters and fellow travelers, but even among its adversaries much indulgence or complacency. There is no doubt that one of the distinctive features of both *Contrepoint* and *Commentaire* was that these journals had no place for indulgence or complacency toward communism. And I should add that this hostility to communism was inseparable from a sustained effort to understand its nature.

Another distinguishing feature of *Commentaire* was that its authors were often professionals, diplomats, and civil servants. We addressed and we published distinguished government officials and professionals, who have limited taste for the "intellectual life" as the French like to conceive this. I believe that, if there was one thing we all shared, it was that we would have considered it a humiliation to be considered an "intellectual."

Another distinguishing feature of *Commentaire* from the beginning was our great interest in international relations and military questions. This reflects at once Aron's activities and the interests of the principals of the journal. I believe that, for anyone who wants to study, for example, the history of international relations, in particular relations of Europe with the United States, and the relations between the United States and the Soviet world, as well as questions of nuclear strategy, *Commentaire* is a very good source that provides a wealth of documentation. We enjoyed, and the journal still enjoys, a special relation with Americans, not only with Allan Bloom and his friends, but with Stanley Hoffmann, with Brzezinski, with Wohlstetter—in a word, with the "establishment" of international relations professionals in the United States. This gave *Commentaire* an advantage as to competence in these questions, which had long been neglected in our country. There was a period when Aron was, if not the only, then in any case one of the very rare thinkers, to deal with questions of strategy, with military questions, by connecting them with international relations and with more general political questions. *Commentaire* certainly remains faithful to this inspiration.

You emphasize Commentaire's *anti-communism. Was the journal not more generally part of a larger movement of the period, that is, the anti-totalitarian movement common to* Libre *[Free],* Esprit *[Mind/Spirit], and then, beginning in 1980,* Débat *[Debate]?*

Why were these journals born at about the same time (though it is rather a matter of a new direction in the long history of *Esprit*)?

It is well known, as I have noted, that France was decisively affected in its very heart by the establishment of a very powerful communist conviction. This was, of course, centered in the Party, but it ran through society as a whole. And despite all the disappointments and the shocks produced by the various episodes of communist and Soviet life, from the repression of the Hungarian Revolution to the XXth Congress, a certain communist or pro-communist vulgate held sway in France over a long period.

At bottom, with the exception of Aron, who rowed against the current largely alone, a coherent and rigorous critique of communism was hard to find in France. Many people were hostile to communism, but the critique of communism was extremely dispersed and incoherent. There was, for example, an economic critique from the right that blamed communism for its economic inefficiency, as if that was the heart of the communist regime. There was the Catholic critique, which blamed communism for its atheism. There was the more interesting critique of communism as "bureaucracy," best expressed by the group *Socialism or Barbarism*. Still, on the whole, there was no common language for the analysis of the Soviet regime, or more generally, of totalitarianism. What happened in the years in question (late 70s and early 80s) was, it seems to me, the rise and spread of a more general awareness, which brought our generation together, of totalitarianism as an extraordinarily meaningful political phenomenon whose radical character had to be assessed. This was an awareness that, in communism and totalitarianism, some of the most fundamental problems of modern politics came to view.

Thus, at the end of the 70s and the beginning of the 80s, the various threads of the critique of communism came together, took a more coherent form, and a certain general problematic emerged that we can call the problematic of the relations between totalitarianism and democracy. Whereas earlier critiques had tended to focus on parts of communism, so to speak, henceforth the questions of communism as a regime and of totalitarianism as a regime, indeed an unprecedented regime, became central. The question that brought us together at that time, I mean, that was shared by those who were about to found *Libre*, *Commentaire*, and *Le Débat* was (to state the matter a little too simply perhaps), how is it that democracy, the democratic movement that is sweeping modern societies along, in the 20th century produces its opposite and turns against itself? Or, to put it another way, how did the sovereignty of the people issue into its own self-destruction in the complete subjection of the people to the representation of the people?

All that was orchestrated differently by different authors who belonged, moreover, to different generations. There were the elders of the group *Socialism or Barbarism*, especially Castoriadis and Lefort; there were among us Tocquevilleans of the right and Tocquevilleans of the left, but we came together around this theme: totalitarianism as revelatory of the most enigmatic and profound problems of democracy. Thus, totalitarianism, with the threat that it still represented at this time, led us to a radical questioning of democracy—a questioning that involved a kind of trembling of a polarity. This is to say that democracy and totalitarianism of course appear as two opposite poles; these are contrary regimes. And yet, at the same time, totalitarianism is comprehensible only within the context and in a sense, as an effect, or counter-effect, of the movement of democracy.

My sketch must appear very crude, because I am trying to advance propositions that we all shared, that were shared by this whole "anti-totalitarian generation"—a designation no doubt a little too boastful, but we were led after all to elaborate the elements of a political philosophy in what was, in fact, an urgent confrontation with the totalitarian phenomenon. I said above that Hannah Arendt's book, *The Origins of Totalitarianism*, was one of my great reading experiences at the *École Normale*. We were all at that time fascinated by totalitarianism, and this would lead us to be fascinated by the democratic phenomenon.

Beginning in 1977, you belonged to a group for political reflection established by François Furet at the EHESS (School of Advanced Study in the Social Sciences) when he took over its direction. What was the point of this informal group? How did it work?

This was really a very informal group and our objectives were purely intellectual. We felt that we lacked the means necessary to understand the political world in which we were living and to establish criteria of judgment that would make it possible to analyze a political situation and to evaluate a political regime. Thus, for us, it was a matter of acquiring a political education. It was Marx who was blocking our access to the early nineteenth century, a time of such deep reflection on the new society. We had to reconquer this lost or neglected territory by rediscovering a political science that was available but forgotten—what I just referred to as the "liberal political science of democratic society," this science elaborated in the early nineteenth century, a science that bequeathed to us some very fine instruments for understanding our societies.

Thus, each of us chose authors according to his interests and his tastes from among the nineteenth century liberals, and we gave presentations and reviews of our reading for each other over a few years. Tocqueville, Constant, and Guizot were our main references. By "our" I mean Claude Lefort, Krysztof Pomian, François Furet, Pierre Rosanvallon, Marcel Gauchet, Philippe Raynaud, Bernard Manin, and myself. Jacque Juilliard sometimes came, I think. And of course, I am forgetting some.

Were the political sensibilities and the areas of interest of this group complementary for you to those of Commentaire?

Yes, of course! But how shall I explain this? What brought us together in those years, whether we were more of the right or of the left, was the same interest in the question of totalitarianism and the conviction that totalitarianism obliged us precisely to move beyond the right-left polarity that characterizes democratic life. Totalitarianism is neither of the left nor of the right; I am inclined to say it comes from elsewhere; it poses a problem much more radical than the difference between right and left in a democratic regime, such that, in effect, the totalitarian question—that of the relationship between democracy and totalitarianism—suspended the differences that we might have had or that we, in fact, had on other subjects.

That said, as far as this group was concerned, it is clear that I was the only one not coming from the left, since all my friends came from one variant or another along the leftist spectrum, whether it was what one called the new left, or Trotskyism, or a group like *Socialism or Barbarism*. But this was not at all a problem; I was perfectly at ease with them and, apparently, they had no problem with me. All things considered, this was a pretty good example of an intellectual generation that was capable of taking a problem seriously and of treating it with a certain competence and with a common inspiration despite the variety of approaches. Retrospectively, in the work that we did, I see a tight linkage being forged with historical experience. I would not say that we fully accomplished the coming together of historical experience and political science of which I have spoken, but we did, after all, come a little closer to this goal.

Of course, after the totalitarian question lost its political urgency and became, so to speak, just a historical question, each of us followed his own path. But I believe this moment of elaboration of ideas in common was nevertheless meaningful for each of us, and was perhaps not without good effect, let us say, on the self-consciousness of the democracy, the political body, of which we are a part.

PART THREE:
FROM THE MODERN MOMENT
TO WESTERN HISTORY

THE MODERN DIFFERENCE

From 1974 to 1993 you were Raymond Aron's assistant at the Collège de France, *then assistant to Emmanuel Le Roy Ladurie. What were the advantages and the constraints of this position?*

The main advantage was that there was no constraint. Jean-Claude Casanova, who was then on the staff of the Minister of National Education, Joseph Fontanet, had suggested that Fontanet create the position of assistant to Raymond Aron. I was named to this position. The only obligation was to help Aron in his research, and since Aron needed no help, I had no obligations. This allowed me to work peacefully toward my own education, free from any obligation to teach in a *lycée*, while listening to Aron, accompanying Aron, and speaking with Aron. I never managed to form a true intellectual dialogue with Emmanuel Le Roy Ladurie. He was charming, and I was aware of his importance as a historian, but his way of looking at things did not captivate me. This was an encounter that never happened.

Over the years, the fact of not having students, which at first seemed to me an advantage, became more and more frustrating. This is why I was at once very grateful to the Collège de France for having sheltered me so long and very happy to leave it to come to E.H.E.S.S., where I would find interlocutors and students.

Your intellectual project crystalized during your years at the Collège de France. *When did it first take shape?*

It would be hard for me to date the first expressions of my intellectual project because, in retrospect, what strikes me is precisely that this project has always been there in my mind, of course very obscurely at the beginning, but it crystalized very early for me in the person of Machiavelli. Even before having read Strauss on Machiavelli, my interest had centered on Machiavelli as the author who summed up and distilled my torment. I myself am surprised by my obstinance in pursuing this original project, since, still now, I am looking for the answer or for answers to the same set of questions.

How shall I formulate this project that has continually engaged me, which I have never left behind and which I have pursued ceaselessly, for better or worse, from this unspecifiable moment? To put it very briefly, what has kept me going is "the question of the modern difference." It is characteristic of the moderns that they declare themselves moderns and will to be moderns: "Let us be modern, let us be resolutely modern!" *At a certain time, something happened.* At a certain time, Europeans decided to do something new, something absolutely unprecedented, which appeared as the modern, which they called modern and by which they distinguished themselves or separated themselves from everything previous. The very idea of the modern thus refers to a proposition, to a project that was embraced in hope by a larger and larger part of European opinion, to an enterprise that progressively rose in power before winning over all of Europe and finally the whole world. This is just a description. This is what happened beginning at least in the seventeenth century. Something radically new was trying to come forth; then it came forth, defined itself, and imposed itself ever more imperiously.

At the same time or almost the same time, this project raised fears that were equal or almost equal to the hope. One can say, then, that the modern centuries have this quality of being dominated at once by the hope and by the fear of a radical transformation of the human condition—a hope and a fear, moreover, which can be shared by the mind or heart of the same person. But finally, on the whole, the fear and the hope nevertheless define parties. Hope defines the "party of movement," the one that wins, by definition; fear or apprehension defines the party of those who will be overcome, or the disappointed, or the skeptics in the onward march of modernity.

For my part, I am interested in this phase, this period, this moment—taking this term not in a narrowly chronological sense—when something decisive happens, but something that still remains enigmatic today. This is because it is possible methodically to describe the different aspects of the modern enterprise—political transformations, technological transformations, religious transformations—without ever succeeding in dissipating the feeling that the enigma is still there, intact, that there is a secret behind the phenomena that otherwise one knows so well. There is an enigma in plain sight because modernity bursts forth, explodes, takes hold, and triumphs, and yet we wonder what it really means, especially since it presents this ambivalence in that it gives rise to the gravest fears at the same time as the greatest hopes. Human beings in the centuries of modernity deploy extraordinary efforts and means in order to "improve their condition," but they never get past a nagging doubt: what has our success really brought us? Is modern life really a better life, and is modern man really a better human being?

At that time, as I think I have already mentioned, I was dominated by what has been called "the anti-modern sensibility." This is to say that, disposed as I then was, and given my great lack of experience, I tended to align myself with those who were apprehensive about the triumphs of the modern movement, or who regarded them skeptically, without joining any particular school. As you know, the anti-modern sensibility or disposition has taken many forms. There is the anti-modernism of the Catholic Church; the very term "modernism" goes back to a theological context, the encyclical *Pascendi* of 1907, which denounced "the false doctrines of the modernists." There is also an anti-modern disposition in the tradition, which goes back to Swift and Rousseau, that sees in modernity a great machine that is accelerating uncontrollably, a machine that, in the name of the mastery of nature, carries human beings further and further from *their* nature. I have mentioned this theme in connection with Strauss. There is also the Nietzschean perspective that sees in the progress of modernity the rising resentment of the masses who wish to crush all that is great in humanity in the name of equality. There are all sorts of registers within the anti-modern sensibility, but, as far as I can remember, I embraced none of these schools exclusively, even though I clearly aligned myself with this disposition.

From the outset my approach was analytical and intellectual; my intention (to return to my first remarks) was to understand. I did not identify myself with the tradition of anti-modern vituperation, which is not to deny the real merits of this tradition, which has given rise to all kinds of brilliant works: the anti-modern vituperation of Léon Bloy or of Bernanos in its Catholic form, or of course of Nietzsche, even if Nietzsche cannot be reduced to this "crier." I never adopted this tone. Indignation and vituperation are not my register. I sensed a riddle to solve, something enigmatic to understand.

Was Machiavelli the riddle or the solution to the riddle?

He was the riddle who promised the solution to the riddle. From the beginning, as I have said, my inquiry centered on Machiavelli. My first book, which comprised three texts of very unequal length, begins with an essay on Machiavelli that was first published in *Contrepoint*.[2] At that time, I recall distinctly, I was discussing my project with Aron, who regarded it with some skepticism. Moreover, I was signing up with him to write a thesis under the title, *History of the Machiavellian Imperative*. It goes without saying that I never wrote this thesis, but, in a way, I have never ceased writing it. "History of the Machiavellian Imperative"—that sounds a little too *chic*. So what was that supposed to mean?

Machiavelli said: "All right, others concerned themselves with imaginary republics that have never been seen; I'm going to concern myself with the effectual truth of things." To consider the effectual truth of things is to start with the way human beings act, the way they behave, and not the way they should behave. Men behave like this, they have behaved like this, they will behave like this. To teach men to behave the way they already behave is what I call "the Machiavellian Imperative." This seems to be clearly contradictory: if human beings behave in this way, why do they need Machiavelli

2   "Machiavel ou la défaite de l'universel,," *Contrepoint*, no. 17, 1976 ; reprinted in *Naissances de la politique moderne. Machiavel, Hobbes, Rousseau*, Payot, collection « Critique de la politique, » 1977 ; re-edited in Gallimard, collection « Tel, » 2007.

to teach them to behave the way they already behave? You see my point. Now, the topper is that this proposition that seems absolutely conservative, since it speaks of humanity in the indicative (human beings behave in such and such a way), was the beginning of an unprecedented transformation of human life. In brief, the Machiavellian Imperative that was the object of my inquiry, the original riddle that got me started, was this paradox of a description of human life in the indicative mode, a description of political life in particular, that brings about an unprecedented imperative and an unprecedented transformation of human existence. I maintain that there is something that remains profoundly mysterious that continues to justify our questioning.

This questioning that constituted the original motive of my research is one that I have pursued through my work on other authors and on the further developments within this modern project. In effect, this project formulated by Machiavelli of the effectual knowing in transformation of the world developed—at first slowly, then faster and faster—until it formed an extremely powerful intellectual web that envelops and organizes modern life as a whole. In short, starting with the heroic initiative of a somewhat mysterious man, who for a long time was considered to be the devil in person, I was gradually brought to strive to reconstitute the immense architecture of the modern political framework, a framework within which the great notions by which we interpret and organize our lives are deployed with an extraordinary authority: man is determined by society, man is a historical being, man is a being who has rights.

Can The City of Man[3] *be considered the outcome of the first movement of your intellectual project, since this work recapitulates the results of this inquiry on the modern period?*

Yes, it can be seen that way. But movements of thought never have a simple chronology. I elaborated the content of this book over a

3   *La Cité de l'homme,* Fayard, 1994; re-edited Flammarion, collection "Champs," 1997.

very long period of time. Consequently, it is very carefully written, and at the same time, it has a systematic character that is a little deceiving because, over the course of this period, my point of view had begun to change. I was in transition. I was reorienting myself toward a much longer historical perspective, as I had begun to do in *The Intellectual History of Liberalism.*[4] We will come back to this topic.

In *The City of Man*, I offer, in effect, my most rigorous analysis of these modern notions that we were just evoking: society, history, the rights of man. I try to analyze them as carefully as possible and analyze them critically, because, for me, far from being as obvious as they are for the moderns in general, they belong to a founding project whose problematic and paradoxical character I had assessed from its beginning. In this sense, certainly, *The City of Man* is the most complete and systematic form of what I might call my critical analysis of the intellectual framework of the moderns.

Can you say briefly in what way these categories of modern thought seem problematic to you, in particular the sociological point of view that is the basis of self-understanding in our societies?

You're asking me to sum up 400 pages in 20 lines! So be it.

Let us take the formula that seems so obvious and so promising to us: man is the being with rights. The formula ties rights to the individual human being, to *each* human being. In each and every individual human being is the entitled holder and, as it were, the carrier of these rights, the rights of man. Good. By "individual," we mean the individual independently of all association with other individuals, independently of all relation with other individuals. But the very notion of right presupposes society and relation because the very definition of right is to organize society and the relations among its members. Thus, there is a kind of contradiction

---

4   *Histoire intellectual du liberalism*, Calmann-Lévy, 1987 ; republished Hachette Littératures, collection « Pluriel, » 2006.

between the idea of human rights in the very idea of right. That is a problem, isn't it?

You asked me about what I call "the sociological point of view." I have already spoken of this in connection with Leo Strauss, who helped liberate us from it. I can add this. You recall that we encountered the question of human *motives*, the decisive importance of which for understanding the human world I have emphasized. Now the sociological point of view never attains clarity on this question, and so it is condemned to go in circles: *anything* can be considered the "social cause" of *any* human behavior. Why? Because the observer has renounced the obligation to recognize what he has in *common* with the one observed. What he has in common with the one observed is human nature and human motives. One cannot do whatever one wants with human nature, because one participates in it and one must recognize oneself in this participation. One can do what one wishes with "society," because, from the sociological point of view, this merely designates the "place of causality" of human behaviors, a place one can fill as one pleases. Take for example the most brilliant and the most discussed work of sociology, Max Weber's essay, *The Protestant Ethic and the Spirit of Capitalism*. There is considerable symmetry between the clarity, the well-defined character of the effect (the Spirit of Capitalism), and the opacity in the elusive character of the cause, the Protestant ethic. Because Weber is as honest as he is passionate, he is ceaselessly limiting, correcting, even extenuating the thesis that he nevertheless continues to maintain, that is, that asceticism in the original capitalist world derives ultimately from the Calvinist doctrine of predestination. In the end, it is impossible to say not only what Weber has proven, but what it is he set out to prove. The comings and goings of an argument that is otherwise deployed magnificently are based on an axiom the scientific character of which can be summed up as follows: because there is an effect, there must somewhere be a cause.

But it was a mistake to look for the cause because, to be precise, there is no effect. Capitalism represents, to be sure, an unprecedented development, but this takes place within and as an aspect of a profound political transformation, that is to say an unprecedented arrangement of human motives. This arrangement consists in liberating the acquisitive instinct from most of the restrictions that held it back. To connect the doctrine of predestination with the accumulation of capital is an exercise in style in which one can say just about anything. To discern as precisely as possible the place accorded to the acquisitive instinct in the ordering of the political body is less spectacular, but in this way one refers only to common and shared human motives. In short, to anticipate a question that is likely to arise, a political understanding of the Reformation will always be more illuminating than a theological interpretation of capitalism.

I'm afraid I let myself get carried away.

How was this book, The City of Man, *received by critics and by your peers?*

It was not badly received, but it was hardly discussed. I am indebted to Philippe Raynaud, in *Commentaire*, for the only serious philosophical critique in France.[5] More generally, it seems, from the responses that I have heard, that I gave the impression in this book that I was interpreting the modern world as the product of ideas fabricated by philosophers. This was not at all my intention and I have never thought that human beings can be simply "governed by their ideas." This is what I have just objected to in Max Weber: that is, transforming an idea—in this case, a religious doctrine—into a social cause. Once again, what is decisive for me is the question of motives. An idea as such is not a motive. Consider for example *The Intellectual History of Liberalism*, which I wrote fairly early in my journey. There I consider ideas carefully—it is, after all, an intellectual history—but they enter into the historical argument only in relation to a political situation or problem that they formulate and seek to resolve. This political situation or

5   Philippe Raynaud, "De la nature à l'homme, » *Commentaire*, Summer 1994, vol. 18 no. 66.

problem always consists in a certain configuration of human motives: why, how, and who is one to obey? The ideas of political philosophers are only relevant and potentially "causal" insofar as they respond to the situation or the problem and as they are articulated in terms of motives.

For example, in *The City of Man* I studied what is called the authority of history: how in the modern epoch History became the supreme reference and judge of human behaviors and undertakings. This modern idea of history involves a thesis on humanity, the thesis that "man is a historical being." You know, the first thing one learns in the last year of *lycée* is that man is a historical being. This means that man has no nature, that he, in a way, creates himself in history. This is a proposition that, taken by itself, is purely theoretical or philosophical. One can argue about it. But at the same time it is a proposition that carries with it the possibility of profound political and moral effects if it is transposed into schemes of action, and if it is thus articulated in terms of motives.

Totalitarianism, for example, is impossible to conceive and to act upon without the pervasive presence, in modern European consciousness, of this idea that there is no stable human order, that there is no human nature, that humanity created itself in history and thus that a new humanity can be created in history. Marxism gathers adherents as historical materialism, that is, as the science of history. When I study the rise of the authority of History in modern consciousness, I am not looking for the "idea" that would be the "cause" of a given modern development. I am looking for a somewhat rigorous understanding of the content and the genesis of this notion, in order to have access to this new situation of consciousness in which some people experience as self-evident and passionately affirm the absence of any limit to human enterprise that might be grounded in the nature of human beings or of society.

That said, to the extent that, in this book, I emphasize the philosophically unsatisfying character of these organizing notions (human rights, History), I necessarily create the impression that I am making the modern political framework the cumulative result of various philosophical errors.

SEEING THINGS POLITICALLY

At the time I was finishing *The City of Man*, I had not yet worked out an interpretation of our political history that was truly independent of the modern conceptualization that I criticized or rejected. I would not succeed in resolving this difficulty till I was able to propose an interpretation of the development of Europe not centered on the modern project.

In my defense, all, or almost all, the interesting work in philosophy and social science in the modern epoch has been, in a way, obsessed with the question of the modern difference. Heidegger is always talking about it, Strauss as well, although in quite different terms, but also Marx and Max Weber, thus a good part of the social sciences. This obsession has two causes. One is the still enigmatic character of the modern rupture, and one cannot abandon the search for a solution to the riddle. The other is the fact that the interpretation of the modern difference is the object of a fight between the moderns and the anti-moderns; it is a *Kampfplatz*, and the combatants do not want to let it go. And what displeases me in *The City of Man*, or, in any case, what has become quite foreign to me, is the excessively polemical posture that risks preventing the reader's access to what is essential in the argument.

In 1982 you devoted a monograph to Tocqueville: Tocqueville and the Nature of Democracy.[6] *Do you still believe it is this author who best illuminates the modern condition?*

He is the thinker who best illuminates the modern condition insofar as this condition relates directly to our political and social regime. He is the thinker who best illuminates democratic life precisely insofar as it is and considers itself democratic. In *Tocqueville and the Nature of Democracy*, I considered only an aspect of Tocqueville's work, but this was the aspect that seemed to me by far the most interesting, in any case, for my own research.

6   *Tocqueville et la nature de la démocracy,* Julliard, collection « Commentaire. », 1982. Republished Fayard, 1993 ; republished Gallimard, collection « Tel », 2006.

As you know well, Tocqueville feels that he is in the presence of a great moral and political revolution, a revolution that today we would call anthropological. He feels that a new type of human being is appearing on the scene, a human being very different from those who have preceded him—very different from our fathers, as he says. With an extraordinary acuity, delicacy of attention, and evocative capacity, he describes this new human being, the being we have become or that we are still becoming.

What distinguishes this new human being? He looks at himself, at others and at the human world from the perspective of equality, and this perspective gives rise to an unprecedented sensibility that Tocqueville calls the "feeling of likeness" (*sentiment du semblable*). This is a faithful summary of the generative ideas upon which his analysis is based. This summary can fit in three sentences, but over hundreds of pages, Tocqueville lays out all the consequences of this transformation in political, familial, social, and economic life, the relationship between masters and servants, between parents and children, men and women, etc. In this respect, I indeed felt that Tocqueville had seen some very important things, at once before everyone else and more completely and judiciously than everyone else. His description of what we have become, or of what we were in the process of becoming, or of what we were going to become, seemed to me the finest and the most convincing.

This was not Aron's view. He had not approached Tocqueville from this point of view; he had approached him in a more directly political way, as an analyst of associations, liberal institutions, and of American democratic life. As for Tocqueville, the phenomenologist of democratic man, Aron found him suggestive without knowing very well what to do with him. This new human being that Tocqueville described in an unforgettable way, a being centered on himself, pursuing little pleasures, and above him, the state that would soon deliver him from the work of thinking and the trouble of living—Aron appreciated this portrait, and found it very suggestive, but he had his doubts: had we really come to this point?

For my part, I was quite smitten by this description. It seemed to me that it truly gave us access to the profound transformation of the human soul in or by the democratic regime. And in my little book, my aim was only to grasp Tocqueville's perspective on this point as synthetically as possible. I say "only" because there are many other aspects of Tocqueville; he is an extraordinarily rich author, but, for my purposes, this book in a way exhausted Tocqueville.

You were smitten by Tocqueville. Was this not the case for your whole generation?

I cannot speak for everyone, but Tocqueville certainly put his mark on the group that we were forming. We were particularly interested in Tocqueville's analysis of equality, which went beyond or rendered largely obsolete the old debate between formal and real equality: in the new society, master and servant remain very unequal, but, since they consider themselves equals, or see themselves from the perspective of equality, they created between themselves an "imagined equality" that radically modifies the nature of their relations.

It seemed to us that this was a discovery that deserved to be an integral part of the self-understanding or the science of democratic societies. This was indeed a discovery. Tocqueville made it possible to see the transformations of life, of society, and of the human world when this world sees itself from the perspective of equality. Our political ideas might have been quite different in other respects, and we might have disagreed in various ways concerning the interpretation of Tocqueville himself, but with this analysis of equality, we were in the presence of scientific findings that were on the whole incontestable.

There is, in fact, such a thing as social and political knowledge, and this knowledge is elaborated by certain minds that are capable of entering profoundly and impartially into the analysis of the political body and of offering a description that obliges the reader of good faith to concede that perhaps not everything perfectly matches his own perception, but that, in its essentials, this description of what has happened to us, this description of the transformation we have experienced and of what we have become—well, it is pertinent, it is truthful, and it is valid.

Tocqueville helps us very significantly to reconstitute a political science of democratic societies. For me, Tocqueville has been a master; he provided the resources for this reflection, but he was not the guarantor of a new social or political orthodoxy. There are different interpretations of Tocqueville, and in any case, my appreciation of Tocqueville is not exactly what it once was. The fact remains though, that, even if this description of the democratic world does not leave me smitten as it did thirty years ago, it constitutes a "permanent acquisition" for the political science of democratic societies.

What moderated your enthusiasm for Tocqueville?

I was brought little by little to ask myself the following question: by adhering so firmly to Tocqueville's description, was I not allowing myself to be seduced, in the etymological sense of the term, that is, to be led down a path that was distancing me from a perfectly balanced view of what a democratic political body is? This, in effect, was the conclusion at which I arrived. Perhaps Tocqueville, the first to be smitten by the novelty of what was new, allowed himself to be carried away by his own intelligence and his own discernment. Perceiving things so acutely, he sees very vividly what is unprecedented—and his description, I repeat, is in some ways irrefutable—but he concludes that what is unprecedented provides the truth of the whole of the democratic regime, of the democratic life that we experience. It is on this point that I distanced myself somewhat from him, because Tocqueville imagines, like Marx in a certain way, that the human world is susceptible to a deeper transformation than is doubtless possible.

The force of the human soul has perhaps been weakened, or at least modified by the democratic regime and by democratic society, but it has not been annihilated. *Thumos* has not been annihilated. There would not be politicians capable of presenting themselves before us and expending superhuman energy to get elected if the human soul were no longer capable of these feelings or these passions. The relative roles of the various parts of the soul may change with the political and social regime, but still, all the parts of the soul are present, if not active, in every human being.

At bottom, all these great authors—Marx, Tocqueville, Nietzsche—share the same conviction that modern man, whom they otherwise describe, understand, and evaluate differently, is always on the point of an ultimate and radical metamorphosis, that he is about to become a new human being, whether Marx's producer, or Nietzsche's "last man"—or perhaps the "over-man," if over-men are available—or he is going to become the ever-so-depressing democratic man described by Tocqueville. All of these authors finally have the idea that humanity is vulnerable to a kind of final metamorphosis that will put him in a final condition. For Marx, this is overall a glorious condition; for Nietzsche and Tocqueville, with their very different styles, this is a state of degradation.

This was a contagious idea. I have said how my generation and our teachers of the preceding generation—I can name Lefort and Dumont—how we shared the view according to which modern democracy brought about a very deep transformation of human life, of human being, of the human soul, even if this last term would no doubt not be agreeable to my colleagues. Up to this point, all is well. It seems to me, nevertheless, that a number of these authors who focus their attention on democracy have had the tendency, at the same time, to follow the path marked out by Marx, Nietzsche, and Tocqueville, that is, to embrace the idea that, with modern democracy, humanity was arriving at its final form, at its final metamorphosis, and that in modern democracy such as we experience it a final truth of humanity, of the human condition, was coming forth. I believe this is true of many contemporary authors. It seems to me that this is very present in Marcel Gauchet's *The Disenchantment of the World*. And in the case of Dumont, moreover, this is a negative truth, modern individualistic democracy being, in a way, the final loss of the truth, of the social truth. But whether democracy is considered the ultimate fulfillment of the social truth or as the final oblivion of the social truth, modern democracy is somehow ultimate, and everything must be understood in relation to it.

This explains the dominance, in recent decades, of an understanding of our history that sees it going from an order called holistic, in Dumont's language, to an order that can be called individualist, liberal, or democratic. From this perspective, the human world is understood according to the polarity between democracy and its opposite—A and not-A. This is the understanding, to which I had adhered up to a certain point and up to a certain time, that I increasingly contested, and from which I have distanced myself more and more, precisely because this is an understanding that seemed to me more and more to be excessively dominated by our belonging to a democratic regime that we could not help considering the final regime of humanity. The great reconstructions that flow from this vision and lead us from holism to individualism, from heteronomy to autonomy, seemed to me more and more to be prisoners of our own confinement within democracy.

As interesting as our democracy is—as interesting as we ourselves are—it is an episode in a history that has known other metamorphoses, including metamorphoses that were doubtless much more disruptive than the transformation of the French *ancien régime* into modern democracy. To give only one example, the creation of the Greek city from existing "families" seems to me to imply a much more important and radical anthropological transformation than the transition from the *ancien régime* to democracy. In any case, the latter was only a weak repetition of the first metamorphosis.

By freeing yourself from this fascination for modern democracy, were you thus led to reconsider the quarrel between the ancients and the moderns?

I widened my field of vision. At least, that is my impression. I came to see the modern project—the "great transformation"—as an episode, to be sure a significant episode, but only an episode in a political and spiritual history, and not necessarily its center, if indeed it has a center. In this sense, my subsequent approach consisted in resituating the quarrel of the ancients and the moderns within a longer and more comprehensive history.

At bottom, what bothers me in the approach of certain contemporaries I have mentioned, such as Louis Dumont, but also in an author like Heidegger, is that their thought is dominated by a polar configuration that is finally polemical. Before our eyes, we see displayed a kind of gigantomachy between the new and the old, but the new and the old are always understood in opposition to each other: modernity is defined by the negation of antiquity, which itself is defined by a kind of anticipated negation of modernity.

Consider Heidegger, for example, even though I hesitate to speak of an author who protects himself so effectively against objections by using a vocabulary known only to himself. But let me try to say in ordinary words what seems to be his typical approach—without claiming to grasp what he brings that is most radical. Whether it is a question of being or of language, Heidegger observes a loss over a long process by which Western man considers himself and conducts himself more and more as if he were the creator and the master of language, the creator and the master of being. In order to overcome this loss, Heidegger reverses the modern proposition or perspective, and he announces that it is language or that it is being that is the sovereign master of man. Here, we see at work what I call the device of polarity and polemics. Now, I have no trouble agreeing that man is the master neither of language nor of being, but this in no way implies that he is its servant, and that the task of thinking is to reconquer, as it were, this subordination. But it is no small task for a magician of language to restore to his own words—through the words of a human being after all, even if their meaning is known to him alone—the very sovereignty of language and of being over humanity!

The solution I speak of thus consisted for me in freeing myself as much as possible from the polemical posture that is common to the two great parties, the moderns and the anti-moderns. And this posture is shared in the last analysis by those who seek impartiality in a polarity that is supposed to be "neutral," "with neither winner

nor loser," between "holism" and "individualism," whose efforts
I have followed with sympathy: they modify the tone, but not the
foundations, of the debate, since it is always a principle of opposition, a polarity between contraries, that organizes their thought.
Opposition and enmity are not only among the most powerful motives in human life; often they penetrate to the depths of thought.
It seems to me that in the most recent period, by reducing, if I may
say, the part of enmity that my thought included, I have attained
an enlarged understanding of the questions that have occupied me
since the beginning.

*To return to Tocqueville's limits, does it not seem to you that Ben-
jamin Constant, whom you have mentioned a number of times,
completes the Tocquevillean description of the modern difference?*

It seems to me that Constant, indeed, complements Tocqueville because he is very sensitive to the irony of the modern condition—
the irony that characterizes the way modern man sees himself. For
Constant, the modern condition is that of reflection, that is, the
fact of seeing himself as another, in a way, and of never being
wholly *in* what one is and what one does.

As you know, Constant applies this diagnosis brilliantly to the
question of love; he considers that modern man is incapable of passion, precisely because he sees himself being affected by passion.
He cannot simultaneously belong to his passion and watch his passion. And since he watches his passion, he always anticipates the
moment it will come to an end. Here, Constant touches, I believe,
on something very profound, on an intimate weakness that affects
democratic man in every aspect of his life: the subject inserts itself
between itself and what it is doing.

This tendency reaches its fulfillment in contemporary art, since
the contemporary artist does not present the work of art, he presents himself as artist; he presents his person as the artist. The work
does not offer itself to be seen; the work of art is the occasion, for
the artist, to present himself as artist. For me, the most apparent
sign of the victory of reflexive irony lies in the recent and extremely

revealing phenomenon of the near disappearance of poetry in the proper sense, even in the case of those who, in other times, would have been great poets. Today we have excellent authors of poetic prose, or poems that lie at the limits of prose—I am thinking, for example (and each will have his own preferences), of Henri Michaux or of Philippe Jaccottet. These authors offer us works that are extremely subtle and of admirable rhetorical competence, but these are always, I would say, works that the author does not allow to achieve independence. He is ceaselessly present in order to comment on the work, to correct it. They bridle themselves severely. I could mention in this context Beckett's *didascalies*, which sometimes take up more space than the text itself. The author *retains* the work at the same time he produces it. And of course, the presence of the author expresses itself as self-mockery. Michaux has an admirable gift for self-mockery. You will remember, for example, when, in *Plume*, he evokes his own disappearance: adieu, Michaux! But if we compare this with what is essential to poetry, and which begins as song, what strikes me is that our poets no longer have the capacity, or in any case the heart, to sing; they no longer have this basic confidence that is the condition of poetry, this confidence in inspiration that makes it possible to throw oneself into song. Was it not, moreover, because of a loss of confidence in the spontaneous fecundity of language that rhyme was abandoned? What contemporary poet would trust in rhyme? No contemporary poet could say what Virgil said to Dante when Dante met him in Hell: "I was a poet and I sang," because our poets no longer sing. My point is not to deplore this state of affairs—when I read Jaccottet I am not sorry he is not Lamartine—but because this seems to me to reveal a very deep transformation of our relationship with language. Even the most gifted of our poets have lost this primordial confidence that is the basis of singing.

When would you say that singing disappeared?

When I speak of poetry that no longer sings, I am thinking of strictly contemporary poetry. French poetry in the 20th century has known two great lyric and epic poets, Claudel and Saint-John Perse, both of whom are gifted with a perfect mastery of the resources of the poetic spirit. They recapitulate very consciously and with great learning the immense melodic wave that carries the inspiration of the West since the days of Homer, Pindar, and Virgil. Recall the leitmotiv of Saint-John Perse's poem entitled *Amers*: "One same wave all over the world, one same wave since Troy . . ."

Why—I pose the question without having an answer—why was the song so suddenly interrupted? Why was the spirit so suddenly lacking? Why are we left with only irony, or, more precisely, with a bitter and satisfied—and of course, very sincere— review of our impotence?

This seems to me, in any case, very revealing of this condition analyzed by Constant, of this lack of confidence in our strength, in our passions, in our convictions and our reason. We do extraordinary things for him. Humanity does all kinds of extraordinary things; it ceaselessly congratulates itself for the extraordinary things it does, and even as we ceaselessly congratulate ourselves for the extraordinary things that we are doing, we ceaselessly and deliberately reduce our capacity of expression. Our humanity, by her own admission, is becoming ever more limited, since, as we say, we can no longer sing, love, understand, believe, or fight, no longer having the confidence in our capacity to sing, love, understand, believe, or fight.

Constant's irony is marvelous, and Michaux's irony is charming, but the cumulative effect, the social effect, of the generalization of irony, is still an ongoing trinket show of human capacities.

Was this not precisely Tocqueville's long-term diagnosis?

Yes, you are right. But up to what point should we extend the curve? I do not think that it is reasonable to envision the extinction of the higher capacities of the human soul. Did Tocqueville himself envision the complete disappearance, or the definitive atrophy, of the aristocratic parts of the soul? He surely thought that great ambitions would become rare, but that leaves us some hope. . . .

Tocqueville is not merely the analyst of democratic man, he is also the one who taught us to see that this man, in order to be understood, must be seen in relation to another type of human being whom he calls aristocratic man. One can have an adequate perspective on the human condition only if one is capable of tying these two perspectives together. Now, of course, to repeat, Tocqueville feels (and here, he is perhaps mistaken) that democratic man will prevail to the point that no trace, so to speak, will be left of aristocratic man. But, in the meantime, what he gives us to consider, what he shows us, is that our societies are at once carried irresistibly by the movement of democratization, by the movement of triumphant equality, and at the same time, they continue to refer to an earlier phase of their social and moral history. In other words, in order to understand ourselves, we need to refer to "our fathers" who lived in different conditions, who lived as "aristocratic men."

In a certain sense, this is just how our Republic understood matters. In effect, if we consider what was republican education, this was an education that strove very deliberately to mingle republican and democratic engagement, education for democracy, on the one hand, and attachment to certain aristocratic requirements on the other. These aristocratic requirements were sublimated and distilled in the artistic perfection of French literature.

It is certainly very striking that the Republic presented its children with an intellectual and literary model taken from *le Grand Siècle*, the century of monarchy and Catholicism, the century of the Court. I was speaking earlier of the importance of French and the education provided by the classic *lycée*. Now, as you know, and as historians of literature have pointed out, it was the king, *le Grand roi*, who settled the usage of the French language. He was the ultimate master of French, the ultimate arbiter of the fine points of the French language in the classic century, when this language found its definitive form. And the Republic took it to heart to teach all the little French children the language of the king. The Republic accomplished something like a mixed regime; it fulfilled the requirement that Tocqueville allows us better to understand.

And you judge this mixed regime to be necessary in the sense that it is a structural element of the order of human things?

It has become clearer and clearer to me, in any case, in moving from liberal political science to ancient political science, the political science of the Greeks, that, if democracy is irresistible, oligarchy is indestructible. The few never disappear or they always regroup. And thus I increasingly felt the need for a science capable of correcting what was still unilateral in Tocqueville's science, subject as it was to the pressure of the experience of modern things.

In short, I adopted a "classic" view of political life, which gives me a better view of the eternal play between the few and the many, beyond the democratic enthusiasm characteristic of modern societies. Here we see, in a way, the difficulty of the science of politics: on the one hand, there is an experience proper to the present time, and one is necessarily exposed to the force of the present moment and to the imperative to give the experience of present things its due; on the other hand, one must know how to resituate these things within the order of human things, the order of things. Where the analysis of modern society is concerned, the problem that I face is thus, to sum up, the following: to hold together Tocqueville's analysis of democracy's power to carry us toward ever greater equality, and the recognition of the eternal play between the few and the many.

Which is entirely forgotten.

Which is entirely forgotten, except in partial and partisan forms: some take the side of the many in the name of an ever more democratic democracy, and some take the side of the few in the name of economic efficiency and fair, unimpeded competition. But the two parties—such is the eternal law of politics—willfully ignore the fact that the few and the many are made to live together and to argue endlessly.

We have learned this, of course, but we keep on forgetting what we have learned. Political science is the most forgetful of the

SEEING THINGS POLITICALLY

sciences. If it were not so, if we were not so forgetful, it would be impossible to understand why, over generations, we thought that the class struggle was an invention of Marx. Marx himself never made that claim; he gave credit for this discovery to "bourgeois historians" such as Guizot. In truth, as Marx well knew, the class struggle shows up throughout the Greek history. There is no doubt, then, that we are continually forgetting. And we must continually re-learn these fundamental principles of political science, which point up the main articulations of political life.

A HISTORY OF POLITICAL FORMS

These fundamental principles, these main articulations that emerge over the long term, are the focus of the second great movement of your intellectual journey. How, beginning with the question of the modern difference, did you come to reconsider the whole political and religious history of Europe?

From the beginning, it was clear to me, and this required no exceptional discernment, that the modern difference, the modern project, was related to religion in a certain way, and first of all polemically and negatively, since Machiavelli, who is pivotal in this history, puts the Christian religion on trial for its deleterious influence on political life. Therefore, anyone who is interested in the modern project and in Machiavelli cannot help but be interested in political and religious history on a large scale, or, to use the now fashionable term, in the theological-political problem.

But on what terms is this theological-political history to be approached? Because my turn of mind is political, and because I look for plausible motives and try to exercise just a little psychological imagination, I wonder why human beings do what they do. I ask myself: is this motive plausible? Can I imagine following such a motive? It is when I begin to be able to answer such questions that it seems to me I am beginning to understand.

On this point, it is clear that, over the course of the 16th and 17th centuries, a set of very simple, powerful, and persuasive motives emerge. The problem of religion and politics presents itself very concretely: who is to be obeyed? Must I obey God, who threatens me with eternal punishment, or princes who threaten me with the death of the body? There is a question that is as urgent as it is interesting. There is a question that is decisive, politically. And when I encounter this question, when Hobbes explains to me that, by claiming a spiritual power, by adding a spiritual power to the temporal power, the Catholic Church is forcing men to "see double," then I think: "This time I understand! This person says something to me, because it must be very annoying not to know whom to obey, not to know which is the legitimate authority in the social space." Here, we can and must recognize one of the decisive articulations of our history.

On the other hand, when I read the very learned histories of philosophy, in which one tends to deduce the whole development of modern politics from the new conception of individuality introduced by William of Occam, then I have to ask myself whether the author is serious—because this does not make sense. It has no human, political, or moral meaning to think that a logical, metaphysical, and analytical innovation, however interesting it may be in itself, could possibly unleash a series of transformations at the end of which human beings had ceased to obey the Church in order to obey princes instead. This kind of historical interpretation is nonetheless always well received, particularly in Catholic circles, because it is always captivating to seek out heresy, and this thesis allows one to deduce an entire historical development from a minuscule theoretical or ontological heresy discernible only to the learned. In any case, I have no more patience for such a view. The springs of human things are ultimately *motives*, and these motives must be recognizable and intelligible for human beings. When Hobbes brings to light the political role of fear, or the link between protection and obedience, he is exhibiting the fundamental *motives* for the construction of the modern state.

To return to my itinerary: I thus applied myself, along with many others, to the study of the history of Europe's theological and political development and, to be very brief, I very soon interpreted European history as that of the response by Europeans to the change in their condition produced by the Christian proposition, or what I call the Christian proposition. In *The Intellectual History of Liberalism*, I began to go back to what preceded the modern rupture: Rome, the empire, and before the empire, the city.

You conceive this long history as a history of political forms. Can you explain, on the basis of the case of the city and the empire, in what sense the interaction of these human associations constitutes for you the driving force of history?

I call this "political form"; it is not necessary to give it this name, but this is the term that seems to me the simplest and most adequate. I am not an erudite historian, and so I tend to look at things from a general point of view. In any case, this is no disadvantage scientifically, because human things tend to arise in a general way; one doesn't need a microscope to grasp them. Thus, if we look at things in a general way, here is what we see: there is an ancient world—let us say the Greco-Roman world— in which we can distinguish two main forms of human association, namely, the city and the empire. And here we must add immediately that the city is the new form of the ancients, the form invited or produced by the Greeks, while the empire obviously refers first to non-Greek empires, the Asiatic empires. The invention of the city, moreover, takes on a revolutionary and positive meaning: Greeks are free, Asiatic peoples are slaves.

The history of the ancient world is, at bottom, the history of the interplay between these two political forms. It is either the story of war between these two political forms, Greek cities against the Persian Empire, or it is that of the passage from one of these forms to the others, that is, from city to empire. Athens was an imperialist city, but it did not succeed in constituting an empire, or in any case in maintaining one; it was Alexander, who came from the periphery of the Greek world, who constituted the Greek Empire. This creates a Greek imperial sphere that will soon welcome a newcomer: Rome. Rome presents us with a different kind of case, since, in the case of Rome, it is the city itself that gives birth to the empire, the city itself that experienced this extension, that applied this almost unbelievable effort to transform itself from a small city into a world empire.

I began with these very simple facts available in any elementary history book. And at the same time as I was attentive to the factual linkages, I noted as well that these political forms, far from being contingent, displayed a very marked character of intelligibility, and that one could say they were on the whole "natural." The city is the smallest human association capable of self-government, of autarchy. Empire, on the other hand, is the most extensive possible assembling under a single sovereign. Thus we have two conceptions of humanity, two ways of crystallizing the fact of being human—a group small enough and large enough to govern itself, and the assembling of the whole of humanity, or at least the greatest possible number, under a single power. The pagan order, the ancient order, is an order that rests on these two great political forms and their interrelations. This pagan order is the "natural" order of human things, to the degree that these two modes of human association developed spontaneously, that is, in the absence of any prior idea or conception (unlike the modern state, for example), and that they correspond at the same time, as I have said, to two very well-defined intelligible types.

We must ask simple questions. We are struck, in considering European history after the fall of Rome, by the persistence of empire: the Germanic Holy Roman Empire, the French Empire, the German Empire, and contemporary Europe, which many speak of as the new empire. And yet it was not these empires that gave Europe its form. Similarly, there have been brilliant examples of the city in Europe, whether in Italy, in Flanders, or in the Rhineland. But European life has not been organized mainly in cities. In any case, this has not been the dominant political form.

In *The Intellectual History of Liberalism*, I began with this fact and wondered about it: just what happened? Why were the two natural forms of human association gradually set aside? And why was a third form finally victorious, a form without equivalent in the ancient world, that is, the nation? Even with all the prestige that was associated with the city on the one hand and the empire on the other, European life was finally organized in a political form that was neither the city nor the empire. Why, and how was this so? There, in simple terms, are the problems that I encountered.

Let me return briefly to the question of simplicity that is so important to me. I have nothing against scholarly notions; they are indispensable. But a scientific thesis *on human things* of which at least the main points cannot be formulated in natural language, that is, by using notions and words common to social and political life, is for me *scientifically* unsatisfying, whatever other merits it may have. By identifying a process that rests on political forms, I propose a history that I can recount in French: the city, the empire and the nation got their names from political life itself. It ought to be possible to recount the political history of humanity, if not to children, at least to plain citizens. Once again, what matters to me in this is scientific integrity or rigor, not what facilitates diffusion or practical utility. A political history that cannot be recounted in the ordinary language of political life is not a truly rigorous history, for it takes shortcuts by making up its own language.

A moment ago you were explaining the deterioration of secondary education by the disappearance of the unifying role of the study of French. Does this same disappearance of a common language also affect the human sciences?

I believe, in any case, that the specialization of language is much less necessary for knowledge of society than it is held to be. Montesquieu, Rousseau, and Tocqueville wrote simply in French. The loss of confidence in the common language is a loss of confidence in the natural intelligence of human beings. Moreover, one can observe a parallel loss of confidence in literature as the refinement of natural language. I cannot emphasize enough that, over the last two centuries, most of the knowledge that society has had of itself has come through literature. It suffices to mention Balzac.

We must not underestimate the political importance of literature, which has nothing to do with the political involvement of writers. Historically, by allowing or giving freedom to the members of society, the modern state brought about a development—"the movement of society"—that became more and more opaque because it was more and more removed from public speech; or it would have become more and more opaque if a new kind of speech had not developed and become very influential, that is, what we call literature. We recognize and we misunderstand this fact when we say that "literature is the expression of society." Since society is, in any case, the expression of humanity, it would be better to say that modern literature inquires into human motives, which had become less distinct because they are no longer embedded directly in public speech but are confined to the element of society which receives a public illumination only in an indirect and weakened manner. In short, the artifice of the state protects the obscure movement of society's nature, while literature sheds light on the sources of human conduct. Under these conditions, there is complementarity as well as tension between confidence in the movement of society and confidence in the power of literary speech.

Today, it seems to me, our condition is terribly unbalanced, to the degree that, on one hand, modern confidence in the movement of society has become an exclusive confidence in the movement of "the world," a confidence, moreover, that no longer includes hope in progress. On the other hand, confidence in the power of meaningful speech, in literary speech, has largely dissipated, and such speech has almost entirely ceased to be a political institution, at least in France, since the beginning of the 1960s.

The inflation of specialized vocabularies, far from giving us the means for a more refined and rigorous understanding, multiplies the crutches with which we try in vain to make up for loss of confidence in our capacity to understand and to speak.

Let us return to Rome. You have invoked the singularity of Rome. Could you explain what you call the "Ciceronian moment," and to what degree this discovery modified or enriched your perspective on European history?

If you don't mind, I will first say a word about and on behalf of Cicero who, as I have already indicated, has been terribly mistreated. Now it is Cicero who was truly the first to confront the political problem of the West, that of the viability of the city, that of the "exit" from the city, and that of the passage from the city to another political form. He played a major political role at a time when the city of Rome could no longer recover its republican political cohesion and when another political form was emerging and was about to impose itself, the imperial form. Finding himself in a sort of no man's land between the city and the empire, Cicero is in a way obligated by circumstances to begin to interpret the new situation and to try to respond to it. He had learned Greek philosophy, he had learned the classical interpretation of the republican regime in which he lived, the notion of a mixed regime, of a good mixture of monarchy, aristocracy, and democracy. That is all very well and Cicero accepts it. The problem is, though, that all that has ceased to work in the framework of a Rome that has been enlarged and distended, a Rome that has burst through the limits of the city. Cicero thus finds himself caught up between ancient notions, which he has moreover undertaken to explain to his compatriots, and the emergence of something new—new, because, to repeat, there is something extraordinarily new that is going on in Rome since, for the first time, this is a city, that is, the most compact and dense political form, that is extending itself to the point of tending to embrace the whole world. Here is a challenge for thinking and a challenge for political action. As we know, as far as action is concerned, Cicero lost his life due to this situation. But we are especially interested in his thought, in the way in which he tried to adapt ancient categories to a new world.

If we read the political works of Cicero, which often come down to us mutilated, but of which, all the same, we have some large intact pieces, we realize that he subjects classical Greek political philosophy to a profound transformation, and that certain doctrines or themes that we are tempted to associate with properly modern political philosophy are already present in his work. (It is not surprising that certain aspects of his teaching are borrowed from the "stoics"; ancient stoicism was already confronting a political order that was no longer essentially civic.) Here are two examples of his innovations: Cicero defined the magistrate as one who "bore the public person," yet the notion of a public person was unknown in the Greek city; and he defined the function of the political order as that of protecting property, which was a definition equally foreign to the Greeks. And one might raise a third point: Cicero insists on the individual form of each person, on his particularity, distinguishing between the common nature of humanity and the nature proper to a person and inviting each person to follow, not only nature in general (as prescribed by classical Greek philosophy), but especially *his* nature.

If you consider these elements together, you see that they imply a profound reconsideration of Greek political philosophy, a reconfiguration that aims to take account, in new terms, of the new situation. Once the evident givenness of citizenship is lost, a person henceforth has two natures, and one's particular nature, which the Greeks did not recognize as such, takes on authority in the public space among the Romans. The definition of political order as the protector of property, of course, once again gives first place to private things—the *res familiaris*—at the expense of the public space. Finally, political things lose the real and substantial character that they had when the city was a whole that was visible as such; henceforth, the extent of the political body is too great, and the whole of the public splendor is concentrated in the person of the magistrate.

All these innovations suggest that Cicero is aware of and, up to a point, encourages what might appear simultaneously as a decomposition and as a recomposition of the civic political order, that he is sketching the outline of a new order, but that these elements are not sufficient to make up a synthetic doctrine capable of grounding or of inspiring a satisfactory new order. By satisfactory I mean capable of preserving something of civic life—what Machiavelli will call the *vivere civile*, or the *vivere politico*— in a political form that is no longer the city. This indeterminacy of thought is particularly noticeable in *De Republica,* which goes in two opposite directions: on the one hand, Cicero emphasizes the collective wisdom of the Romans throughout their history, to the detriment of an individual legislator like Lycurgus for the Greeks; on the other, he is looking for a monarchical or royal figure, a *princeps* capable of restoring the civic order that the mixed regime, though preferable in itself, is proving incapable of preserving. Thus, if not for the ages, then at least for many centuries, it is Cicero who gathered most intelligently and wisely all the usable elements of the pagan political tradition and transformed them, but still without being able to give them an operational form. He will be the source and the resource of political thought for as many as fifteen centuries. He is a major point of reference for Augustine as well as for St. Thomas. He is truly the source. And his authority, in what we call the Christian centuries, is more or less equal to that of the Church Fathers.

Looking at these centuries, the centuries that precede the crystallization of the modern order or the construction of the modern state, I realized that what best characterized these centuries politically was paradoxically the absence or the indeterminacy of the political order. I have suggested the term "Ciceronian moment" to designate this long period in which the political order is indeterminate. The political order is indeterminate because it has not found its political form. Neither the empire nor the city is capable of meeting the demands of the new situation. The regime is also indeterminate, because the received doctrine of the "best regime" is of little help when the political form upon which it was based is no longer available. The only political teaching that remains relevant is Cicero's, with the strengths and limits that I have just briefly indicated.

We thus find ourselves confronted with a considerable number of centuries that, in a way, we don't know what to do with. I say "we don't know what to do with" because, though we know many things about these centuries, we cannot find in them the deployment of a coherent human order.

We have a coherent view of the ancient order, the Greek and then Roman order, insofar as it possesses coherences in civic life. The uncertainty emerges in the passage from the city to the empire, an uncertainty to which Cicero strives to respond. Then we have an understanding of the modern order that the new is all the more complete because the modern state was built on a foundation that can be said to be philosophical. So we have these two major periods of intelligibility. Moreover, if we look at the histories of political philosophy, it is clear that there is the great grouping of the ancients, and then there is that of the moderns, and then there is a long period between the two that we do not know what to do with. Thanks to the academic division of labor, you can easily find nice scholarly volumes dedicated to medieval political thought, but if you get into the subject matter you are struck by this: the thought of medieval authors is divided essentially between a part that extends ancient thought or that derives from it and a part that announces or prepares modern thought. Of course, we have seen a "rehabilitation of the Middle Ages," which is a very good thing, but the recognition of the accomplishments of this period must not cause us to overlook what is decisive from a political perspective: this period does not lend itself to a coherent understanding of the human world because it had no access to any passably coherent human order.

Since thought hates what is indeterminate, we are tempted, irresistibly as it were, to fill this void with something that seems to us to settle things. So we might say: "this was a period of the great agricultural revolution." This is not false. Or we might say: "the Middle Ages are the ages of faith, the period in which the church governed, or at least ordered the common world. The Middle Ages are fundamentally the age of ecclesiastical order, or of an order governed by the ecclesiastical model." I have already shared with you my skepticism concerning the notion of an age of faith. In any case, the papacy's incapacity to produce a political order is one of the best documented facts of European history. It would thus be curious, to say the least, that Europe was for centuries governed, even indirectly, by an institution incapable of governing.

What I suggest is that it would be judicious to accord major importance to what I would call, in Aristotelian terms, the privation of order, or to the absence of order, or to the indeterminacy of the political order. My view is that it is important to begin by saying that during all those centuries, Europe was in search of its *political* order. Some great discovery, you might say. It is certainly not a discovery. What I am saying is that here we have the kind of decisive consideration that is sometimes sought in the laborious development of productive forces, and sometimes in the sublime expressions of ontology or of theology. I see in this fact—the privation or the absence of order—a *cause*. The historical cause or historical causality in this "Ciceronian moment" is the disorder of European politics, along with the effort to find some way of escaping it. If one prefers positive terms, we can say that the cause is the need or desire of human beings to be governed and, preferably, to be well-governed or not too badly governed. The source of European development is the desire or the need for a political order that is at least somewhat reasonable, somewhat coherent. The cause of history is humanity's political nature.

Isn't the picture we have of the Middle Ages rather that of a period of order?

This is so true that still today there are English Christian socialists who seek the remedy for the "liberal disorder" in the "communitarianism" or the "holism" of the Middle Ages. There is no doubt that I am going up against a veritable platitude here that is an obstacle to understanding, namely, that the Middle Ages were a period of order *par excellence*, that the Middle Ages were characterized by an order that was coherent and even splendid, embracing the cosmos, God and man, and of which the great and visible expression is found in cathedrals. I admire cathedrals as much as anyone, but to make them the symbol of the order of an age is really to get off on the wrong foot for understanding what happened. I am always surprised to see to what point even learned opinion is moved by images, subjugated by images that flatter the imagination but that have no relation to the life of the people of which one intends to give an account. Such is the power of the image of cathedrals, which are of course splendid, or of Dante's *Divine Comedy*, this great and perfect poem. It is crazy how the *Divine Comedy* has served to justify this representation. This is all the more ironic since Dante had given his own work the simple title *The Comedy*, and since, if one actually reads this work, one gets quite a precise idea of the profound political *disorder* of this period.

In the first place, there is this rivalry between the papacy and the political powers that so preoccupies Dante, and that is, moreover, very well-documented. Furthermore, the political powers themselves are fragmented, dispersed among empires, kings, princes, lesser lords, cities more and less free, etc. Thus, there is an extraordinary fragmentation in the medieval world, a fragmentation that of course extends to the principles of common life. The emblematic figure of the medieval order—the "Knight of the Middle Ages"—is a figure of the confusion of principles. This was a composite figure in that there was a very strong tension between his religious vocation and his vocation as a warrior—even leaving aside his possible vocation as a lover—since he was at once a man-of-war and a man of the church or a man of Christ. This tension plays out in exemplary fashion in the Crusades, which were at once a manifestation of European energy and an expression of European confusion. It is clear that the movement to go liberate Christ's tomb, as Hegel famously observed, embodied a confusion between the mediate and the immediate: the Crusades had not yet understood that Christ offered himself to human interiority and that the material conquest of the empty tomb did not give access to grace or to salvation. The massacres of Jews that the Crusades brought about were another expression of the same confusion: by the physical destruction of the "old Israel," it was thought possible to assure "immediately" the exclusive legitimacy of the Church, the "new Israel."

The Middle Ages are thus a period of very deep disorder, from which it will take Europeans a long time to free themselves. I am

SEEING THINGS POLITICALLY

not saying that there are not admirable things in the Middle Ages—after all, I am still half-Thomist. I am not putting the Middle Ages on trial. But politically, what is decisive is that this was a time of disorder. It follows that the traditional representation, which is very dear to a certain Catholic tradition, and which consists in saying: "there was a beautiful order of the Middle Ages and then there was the outbreak of the modern disorder"—it follows that this is politically false, for exactly the contrary is true! There was a medieval disorder that the moderns progressively overcame in order to establish a certain order. It is possible to prefer medieval disorder to modern order ("Toward the Middle Ages enormous and delicate / I would my weary heart in grief might navigate / Far from these days of carnal joy and pleasures sad," Verlaine said[i]), but there is no doubt that the moderns sought and found order. Our societies are incomparably more coherent and orderly than medieval society. It is possible to say, if one insists, that they are the worse for it, but in any case, if we are speaking of order, then we are the people of order. It is the Middle Ages that are disorder, and it is modernity that orders, and that orders very systematically with the construction of the modern state, and then with the construction of the homogeneous modern nation. The vector of modern development, as Guizot saw very well, is the construction of an ever greater generalization starting with the almost unlimited particularity that characterized medieval society.

Catholics are not alone in seeing this age as an ordered whole.

That is what is amusing in this history, and what makes for a kind of quasi-unanimity in the historiography. The great traditionalist Catholic account, that is to say, "we went from the beautiful medieval order to the liberal individualist disorder," has been entirely assimilated by the modern social sciences and historical anthropology, with a simple inversion or neutralization of signs. The reactionary proposition is, henceforth, modulated as follows: "we were not in a beautiful medieval order, but in a holistic order—note the neutral, thus scientific term—and now we are in an individualistic order (optional corollary: this individualist order marks the fortunate culmination of human efforts)." In other words, the "value judgments parentheses" or the coloration of the argument has changed, but traditionalist reactionaries, liberal individualists, and neutral sociologists or anthropologists are in agreement on this false thesis: the medieval order is an order, and a holistic order.

It is not for lack of trying, but I have never been able to understand how human beings could pass from a holistic order to an individualistic order. It cannot be the same human being that produces and orders its humanity according to such opposite forms. Or else we must admit a *common cause* for the two orders. But then this common cause would be the source of intelligibility. It is, in any case, this common cause that I seek. And since we are dealing with human things, this common cause is a common motive: the need or the desire to be (well-) governed. As I have already indicated, in this way, I put myself in a position to understand a profound historical change, which is nothing less than the construction of the modern political order, starting with a general and verifiable proposition on human beings in general.

I must immediately add that this universal human need for order or for good government expresses itself in Europe in a context defined by two specific conditions. The first is obviously the pagan political experience of civic life and of the difficulty or the impossibility of recovering civic life once it has been lost, that is, the "Ciceronian" experience. The second is the Christian proposition of a human community at once more extensive and narrower than any political community, a proposition that necessarily put in question the legitimacy of the two great pagan political forms, the city and the empire. In Europe, the human desire to be well-governed is sharpened and complicated by this double condition.

Did taking into account this long "Ciceronian moment" that precedes modernity lead you to reinterpret Machiavelli's project?

No, I do not have a different reading of Machiavelli, even though, of course, I hope to have made some progress in my understanding of the enigmatic gentleman. From the outset, I was aware of the intensity of his hatred for the Church and in truth for Christianity. This seems to me settled. I am more aware of the importance of the situation of political indeterminacy that I have just emphasized: it is Machiavelli who *replies* with the most audacity to the situation. To speak of indeterminacy is to say concretely that all political forces are weak. Strong monarchies, such as the French or Turkish monarchy, are beginning to arise, but in Italy, there are only weak forces. The Church is strong in a sense, but its strength only serves, according to Machiavelli, to prevent the unification of Italy.

What, then, is Machiavelli's project? Upon what political form, old or new, does he intend to rely? On the old city, a new nation *à la française*, or a new empire? The answer is not clear, any more than the structure of the new regime he envisions. What is certain, on the other hand, is that he conceives the idea of an ever-possible *action*. I do not claim here to propose an interpretation of his thought, but in order to resituate Machiavelli within my problematic of the "Ciceronian moment," I would recall this: with his idea of the virtuous prince, of the prince endowed with virtue, a virtue that consists in being capable of mastering fortune, of taking on fortune and triumphing over it, Machiavelli is opposing the inertia of a political and religious order that knows only how to prevent itself from attaining the perspective of an action that must always be possible. This is Machiavelli's basic tonality: nothing must discourage us; action is always a possibility; fortune smiles on the audacious as do women on enterprising young men. And he defines a certain number of conditions of this possible action; he sets aside religious or moral obstacles to this possible action, without yet clearly outlining the new order that this action is supposed to produce. He never ceases to evoke the *ordini nuovi* that he recommends, but these "new orders" do not really make up recognizable institutions. They are to institutional construction what the preparation of artillery is to battle. Machiavelli sets aside, discredits and refutes all moral and religious precepts, all maxims of prudence, and all the forms of respect that are transmitted with mother's milk that might prohibit, restrain, slow down, or discourage action. To the maxims of morality, he opposes his own, the "Machiavellian" maxims, these deliberately shocking maxims intended to awaken man from their passivity and from the inertia induced by the idea of a good action, since nothing restrains action more than the idea of good action. There you have it. Machiavelli posits the necessary conditions for the possibility of a new order. And for a new order to be possible, Europeans must believe that a creative action is possible, that a founding action is possible, that it is time to forget the old Greek, Christian, and even Roman foundations, in favor of new foundations, as powerful or more powerful than the ancient foundations.

If Machiavelli were a theologian, one might say that he reduces the theological virtues to a single one, that is, hope. If you are a moral philosopher, one might say that he reduces the cardinal virtues to a single one, namely, courage. What I want to bring to the fore, is the fact that he preaches a new political action, a radical, unprecedented, transformative, and founding action, and he preaches it outside of any available or even projected political order. This is an action that will create the conditions of possibility of all possible action. The new order remains somewhat indeterminate, but Machiavelli elaborates a perspective and cultivates a sensibility that might be called revolutionary. The term is overused; we have known many revolutions, and in fact, revolution has even become the most hackneyed of advertising slogans. But here it is serious; it is very serious, because one can say that with Machiavelli, for the first time in Europe, we hear the call to revolution.

The Reformation was another pivotal moment in the theological-political history. To what degree does it illustrate the relevance of your approach in terms of political forms?

I can here approach this subject only from its political angle. Of course, the Reformation has, first of all, a religious or spiritual meaning, but there can be no doubt, I believe, that the Reformation also presents itself very immediately, very directly, and very explicitly as a political movement in the large sense, since it is a movement that bears on the human association, on the relationship between the mind or spirit and the human association.

The heart of the Reformation is undeniably its contestation of the mediating character of the Catholic Church. The Catholic Church offered itself as the necessary vehicle of salvation and the necessary mediation between man and God. The difficulties involved in this mediation are well known. Luther attacks this mediation very directly and very violently, and the destruction of ecclesiastical mediation will bring about profound political upheavals.

The break with ecclesiastical mediation in effect gives practically all power, including a certain spiritual power, to the temporal prince, since the Reformation strips spiritual princes or spiritual powers—the Church and the prelates—of their legitimacy. It is the community of citizens, if we dare refer to them already in this way, or the community of believers, that is henceforth the depository of religious authority; and since the community of believers is governed by temporal princes, it is the temporal princes who inherit the mediating power. Thus, the first political consequence of the Reformation is this: a considerable increase in the power and authority of temporal princes.

There is a second consequence, which is also very visible from the moment of the Lutheran rupture: if it is not the universal Church that constitutes the spiritual community, if the Church does not have the intrinsic substance that it claims to have, then the sacred community, the Christian community, is the community as defined politically and temporally. Now, the community defined politically and temporally is the national community. We know to what degree the Lutheran Reformation was a national revolution, if I may use this expression. This was a German revolution, and the Germans will long feel nostalgia for this great German Lutheran revolution "that had no sequel," in Fichte's regretful words after the French Revolution.

Thus, we already see, and this is no small thing, that the break with Catholic mediation contributed to the strengthening of elements that will be decisive in the constitution of modern Europe, that is, the sovereignty of national princes and the authority or force of the national principle. We will never know how Machiavelli would have appreciated the political consequences of the Reformation. In any case, it contributed powerfully to the destruction of the inertial factor he deplored, that is, the political impunity of spiritual princes. The destruction of Catholic mediation lies at the basis of an active coming together of temporal princes and Christian peoples. Such is the power of negation.

In short, understood politically, the period of the Reformation is the period of the nationalization of Christianity. The secular community becomes directly, immediately religious. Secular institutions—work and marriage—are delivered from competition with spiritual institutions, that is, contemplative orders and consecrated celibacy. The Catholic Church was essentially a brake on human activity; it tended to dissuade people from doing whatever they might do in this world. With the Church pushed to the side, the elements of the social world tend to take on accelerated movement. Calvinist countries will often, in fact, be at the head of the economic social and political movement. As far as religion is concerned, the essential factor in the acceleration of this movement resided in the destruction of the braking effect of the Church's mediation. So it seems to me, with all due respect, that Max Weber makes things more complicated than they need to be when he tries to connect the spirit of capitalism with the consequences of the Calvinist doctrine of predestination— the Puritan entrepreneur, a worldly ascetic, looking for the sign of his election in economic success. This doctrine is in itself obscure; its effects on the soul that embraces it or is subject to it can be so diverse, and, as I have already emphasized when I criticized the sociological point of view, the relationship between the doctrine of the believer and the action of the agent requires so many intermediate hypotheses that it is hard to form a clear idea of what Max Weber intended to establish. Is there not, moreover, a display of virtuosity in the effort to connect such a powerful and general movement, a movement the motives of which any human being can understand by looking in himself or around himself, to a theological proposition no theologian has been able to render plausible, much less attractive? Why connect a movement so *general* with a cause so *particularizing*?

And this brings us back to the question of simplicity. Just as my recourse to the "Ciceronian moment" presupposed no more than the simple and verifiable proposition that human beings would rather be well-governed than badly governed, similarly, the interpretation of the meaning of the Reformation is based on the simple proposition that, structurally, the relationship of mankind to the divine—whether the divine exists or not—involves a problem of mediation. The logic of the relation of humanity to divinity is deployed in two opposing directions: on the one hand, we wish to arrive at a sound idea of divinity, an idea that is adequate and worthy of divinity, and thus, it's we who distance it as far as possible from man. This is divine transcendence. On the other hand, we necessarily wish to enter into a relation with this transcendent God; thus the quest for mediation. As you see, I am careful to proceed in such a way that historical causality is always tied to non-historical causality, that is to say, to something that simply belongs to the human condition. This is neither the condition of the Greeks, nor that of the Romans, nor that of the Christians, nor that of the moderns, but simply the human condition. There is in the human condition a certain relationship with the divine and, therefore, a problem of the mediation of the divine, just as there is a problem of government. These are simple problems, which can be formulated in simple terms. They can also be formulated in refined terms, but they are simple problems that are encountered in these simple terms by living human beings. These are not problems that can only be formulated by specialists in social sciences, or logicians, or theologians.

You are looking for historical motives or causes that are valid for human beings as a whole. And yet you do not deny the influence of political forms and regimes on human types and political virtues. Do you think, for example, that a person involved in politics today could imitate or even understand Cato's suicide?[ii]

Your question leads me to correct or, at least, to be more precise about what I just said. Thus, I insisted on what we might call the requirement of universality: the motive invoked to explain any human conduct in a given society must, in principle, be comprehensible to any human being and thus find some basis and confirmation in his experience. So you are right: Cato exemplifies the problem of social knowledge, or of moral and political knowledge, because his conduct is the object of an ongoing questioning and perplexity. Roman suicide in general has something that is especially troubling for us; whatever our efforts of moral imagination, we have trouble identifying with this action. Our "dear Romans," as Montesquieu would say, leave us here before an enigma.

The interpretation of the figure of Cato has long been a kind of classroom question, one might say, in the history of European moral and political philosophy. Why is this? Cato represents Republican virtue. We can start here. And Republican virtue is virtue of a man who stands up for himself, it is virile virtue. The question that arises is the following: to what degree does this virtue suffice unto itself? To what degree is this virtue always possible? Or to what degree is this virtue tied to a particular political form and a particular political context?

In the case of Cato, the question is raised whether he was perfectly virtuous, or whether, perhaps, there was something false and illusory in his virtue. Cato is, of course, admirable, but at the same time there is something vain in his virtue, since the republic that it was supposed to maintain, animate, give life to, was already definitively dead. We thus remain in uncertainty, and we wonder whether Cato's virtue is the culminating expression of human virtue or whether, finally, his suicide is a not-so-admirable self-regarding act, in that it manifests his refusal to bow before Caesar. Does Cato represent Republican virtue, the summit of human virtue, or is his suicide the effect of a dominating private passion?

This figure of Cato, or this figure of republican virtue, will continue to haunt European history, because what is at stake in it is the very possibility of an unequivocal and simply human affirmation of humanity or of human virtue. Does Cato, this great republican citizen, represent the pure and simple fulfillment of humanity, or is his fate linked to a particular, limited and thus in the end, obsolete form of humanity? The figure of Cato accompanies the long "Ciceronian moment." As I have just recalled, it did not escape much questioning and indeed suspicion, but in the end, it was he who wanted to hope against all hope that the republican order is possible, and there was passionate interest in Cato as long as the belief persisted that this order was, if not perhaps still possible, then at least desirable. The interest in Cato comes to an end with the end of the "Ciceronian moment" and at a time when republican virtue no longer defines human excellence. The Republican reference was left behind, or it was very profoundly modified over the course of the 17th century with the definitive renunciation of Rome as a political example and with the effort to reconstruct the political edifice *de novo* on the basis, not of the active citizen, but of the rights-bearing individual.

On this point, I would like to add a remark concerning Montaigne. La Boétie and Montaigne represent an extraordinarily powerful and brilliant expression of what we might call European republicanism. These two are also very great citizens of a republic that has not existed for centuries and, in a way, their friendship becomes a substitute for the city. Montaigne very explicitly presents their friendship as a Republican conspiracy.

As we know, their friendship lasted only four years, since La Boétie died very young. Montaigne later said of his life that "it was no more than a dark and troublesome night." After the premature death of his friend, who was thus unable to pursue the great political projects that Montaigne suggests were of an audacious and even revolutionary character, Montaigne is led to ask himself if one can be a great citizen without a city. This explains his unfailing interest in the figure of Cato, whom he finds admirable because he showed men all their nature can do. For this, we can overlook his tendency to be "always on his high horse."

And at bottom, what Montaigne is trying to do in his life and in his *Essays* is to show human nature all that it can be even when the city is no more. Montaigne, for his part, is never "on his high horse," even if he is always in his way "very careful" [French "à cheval," on his horse].

In what way exactly is Montaigne still a republican?

He is a republican in that he aims for this self-affirmation of virile human nature, or this virile affirmation of human nature. Republicanism, in the European tradition, is not simply the choice of a political regime preferable to monarchy. Or, more precisely, if one prefers the republic to monarchy, this is because the figure of the citizen signifies the affirmation of the integrity or of the independence of human nature. Whatever the merits or the possible utility of monarchy, or its necessity in certain circumstances, in the end, it imposes certain constraints and forms of servitude on human nature. In a monarchy, one is under a king, *sub rege*, one is under someone or something. From this point of view, the republic certainly represents the regime of self-affirmation for human beings.

A problem arises when he determines that the ancient republic is no longer truly available for humanity's self-affirmation. From this follows Montaigne's immense enterprise, which I am tempted to characterize as a great enterprise in the privatization of the citizen. Montaigne strives to show how the republican virtues, duly modified, can also be manifest in private life, in a life that is "low and without luster."

Montaigne may be republican, but he has a weakness for Julius Caesar! Does the figure of Caesar take on a particular meaning in your historical perspective?

Caesar is certainly the man whose name alone has the greatest resonance. His is a figure that calls for comparison with Cato since, as I said, Cato, a great citizen of Rome, as was Caesar, does not consent to be at Caesar's mercy. He prefers death.

What makes Caesar's access to supreme power such a striking thing for the imagination, such an extraordinary and strange thing, is that, at the moment of which we are speaking, the regime is changing at the same time as the political form. The republic of great citizens is no longer possible because it is no longer possible to maintain equality among them and because it is thus no longer possible to maintain friendship among them. There is a necessary passage from the government of many to the government of one alone. This is a change of regime. But the framework of the regime has also changed radically, since the city has extended itself considerably, thanks particularly to Caesar's action and his conquest of the Gauls—a conquest that, in its duration, its scope, and its geopolitical consequences was, in a way, a qualitatively different action from all other Roman conquests.

Caesar becomes the only ruler at the moment when the city of Rome, which has been extended indefinitely, gives way and crystalizes into the imperial form. This is no longer simply the victory of one *princeps* over the others. Caesar is not only the winner over his former companions; he is suddenly the ruler of the world, the ruler of the whole of humanity. And who is capable of governing the whole of humanity other than a god? Allan Bloom thus opens his *Shakespeare's Politics* with, "The tragedy of Julius Caesar is the story of a man who becomes a god." And he becomes a god to the surprise and consternation of his old companions.

In the figure of Caesar, we see concentrated not only the main political problem of a free political regime—that is, how to preserve equality between citizens from prevailing over others to the point of dominating them—we also see represented here the other great political problems of European history: the problem of the passage from one political form to another (in this case, from the city to the empire, which embraces the whole of humanity), and the problem of the relationship between humanity and divinity, since, once the empire has assumed its full extent, the emperor can in a way only be a god, or the mediator between men and gods. Thus, in the figure of Caesar, we have at once the question of the political regime, the question of political forms and the question of political and religious mediation.

Finally, Caesar truly became a god, since it was his *name* that governed Rome after his physical death. This again is an extremely singular phenomenon—that the name of Caesar had this power. In a way, there was a kind of metamorphosis or recomposition of Rome that made a single man at once the monarch of a monarchy, the emperor of an empire, and the god or the mediator of a humanity that must find its relation to the divine. The consequence—and this returns us to the question of Cato, but seen from the other side—is that Europeans will never cease wondering how to evaluate the figure of Caesar.

According to what I might call the official doctrine of the European republic, Cato is the hero of the republic and Caesar the founder of tyranny. But this official doctrine has never held up in these simple terms because, in truth, as I have noted, we wonder if the figure of Cato is really as admirable as is said, and we thus wonder whether the figure of Caesar is worthy of condemnation as is said. You are right, moreover, that Montaigne is always going back and forth from one to the other and questioning their virtues. It seems impossible to judge Cato and impossible to judge Caesar, or at least, to grant decisive superiority to one or the other. In the *Divine Comedy*, Dante divides his admiration: if he puts Caesar in limbo, that is, with just men who were lacking grace, Cato guards the entry of purgatory. So Dante favors Cato, it seems, but then what are we to make of the fact that Caesar's assassins are with Judas in the last circle of hell?

It is impossible not to encounter the limits of political judgment when one political form transforms into another, when a regime that was good but corrupt gives place to one that is not as good but in a way necessary, and when the very principles of human order have become uncertain. In this transition, humanity is shaken, I would say, in a way that human beings are not capable of mastering; it is shaken such that the most refined judgment fails to settle matters between Cato and Caesar.

You see, then, that throughout this period I call the "Ciceronian moment," this very long period of seeking the very principles of a viable political order, Europe expresses its uncertainty and its perplexity through its interest in this undecidable quarrel between Cato and Caesar. Rome left us an immense, crushing, and contradictory heritage, which we are unable to inventory. The radical character of the modern enterprise was, in part, the price that finally had to be paid to leave behind this alienating legacy.

PART FOUR:
TEACHING POLITICAL PHILOSOPHY

In 1992 you became a Director of Research at EHESS (The School of Advanced Studies in Social Sciences). Did you feel you had a vocation to be a teacher?

I did not say to myself, "I would like to teach." It simply happened that, after a certain number of years at the *Collège de France*, of which we have spoken, it was natural for me to come here, where I had friends, as well as an intellectual context and working conditions that were altogether favorable. And then, I wanted to come to the School for Advanced Studies because I was invited—by Furet, Gauchet, and Rosanvallon. One might say that this was the natural next step in our history. It was meant to be that we find ourselves together again, at the School for Advanced Studies

François Furet and Pierre Rosanvallon played a major role in my election to the School. You know that there was a kind of electoral campaign. It's complicated. Marcel Gauchet was also very helpful. He and I already shared a close and old friendship. I can date its beginning. He had read my review of Lefort's *Machiavelli*. In 1974, he sent me his own review, which had just appeared in *Critique*. I recall the note that accompanied this review: it was warm and vigorous, with that grave good cheer or cheerful gravity that is Marcel's tone. Soon after, Françoise and I came to live in Paris between *Bastille* and *Nation*, very near his place. Thus began the years when we saw much of each other, generally at my place, where we held long sessions in which we made an inventory of available lines of thought (we were rather severe) and made lists of tasks to accomplish (we were also ambitious). We were in deep agreement on the importance of political things and the radical character of political philosophy. We were truly on the same wavelength. Later, life's circumstances were such that we saw less of each other, and of course, our works took on their respective physiognomies. I do not know what Marcel would say, but after more than thirty years, it seems to me that we have done well enough in ful-filling the program of our youth, each in his own way.

Instruction at the EHESS *takes place in the form of seminars. What has this experience brought you?*

From the beginning, I took the seminar very seriously, and it has become the center of gravity of my intellectual life. Every year provides the opportunity for a new or renewed inquiry, one that must be formulated for direct delivery. This means that every week I present the result of a certain intellectual effort to interlocutors ready to react or respond to what I have to say. This seems to me the only truly living formula. There is something extremely frustrating about the so-called "magisterial" class, precisely because there one addresses an anonymous collectivity. In a seminar, one addresses persons who have chosen this seminar who come, each with his own interests and his own history.

I do not say that the conditions of a seminar are those of ordinary life, but a seminar enters much more into the metabolism of ordinary life than a magisterial class, which necessarily has an artificial aspect because it is constrained by certain set parameters. A seminar is freer, more natural. There is almost nothing institutional about it. It quickly takes on its own physiognomy, and each participant has his name and his face. The seminar is at once and inseparably a place of friendship and a place of intellectual endeavor.

Does the seminar at the School derive its specific character from the fact that it takes place within an institution that has a particular standing within the landscape of French higher education?

The seminar at the School is founded on the idea that research is taught by research, which seems to be an excellent method. The School's principle from the beginning has been that seminars are individual undertakings because they are tied to individual research projects. We do not teach disciplines in the usual sense; each of us has a research project accepted by the School that he then develops as he sees best. And the students or listeners who are interested by this research project follow the seminar and participate in this research. It is by the intermediary of this common activity that teaching is carried on. This is the idea of the School; this is its principle, and it seems to me excellent. It requires some adjustments according to the age of the students, because with the recent arrival of master's students at the school, we are taking students one year earlier, and one year, at that age, is not negligible. This means that some seminars are more teaching seminars than research seminars. But in the end, the principle is essentially maintained. We must hope, further, that this idea of research will be preserved in the future, because we are more and more oriented toward a quantitative and "measurable" conception of research, which is incompatible with the kind of intellectual elaboration that takes place in the seminar. The way a seminar is constituted requires some time, and its intellectual fecundity cannot be evaluated by means of "impact coefficients" calculated by computers. All the evidence suggests that the new means of evaluating research are not favorable to the kind of teaching that we are trying to provide here.

A researcher's influence derives from his work as it is evaluated by his peers and by the interested public, and from his teaching as evaluated by his students. From all this he forms a "scholarly portrait" by which he inscribes his personal signature on his work, and which signifies his contribution as a human being to the scholarly life, a life which is open to the whole of social life. On the contrary, the new quantitative techniques of evaluation enclose the scholar in a bubble the citizen cannot penetrate. Consider how a mediocre article written for a "peer-reviewed scientific journal" contributes to a good rating, while a good book addressed to the public is not taken into account in the new form of evaluation.

Do you think you benefit at the Aron Center[iii] from a kind of freedom that you would not have at the University?

I believe so. First, we enjoy complete freedom in choosing our subjects and pursuing our research. Next, we are a group of colleagues, friends, comrades who, on the whole, while sharing somewhat comparable approaches, also reciprocally and jealously hold to our freedom. We share the same conception of free intellectual activity. Consequently, none of us would consider introducing more "governance" than is necessary, and we have succeeded up until the present in preserving complete freedom.

You have also taught for a long time—about ten years— in the United States, at Boston College. What left its mark on you in this trans-Atlantic experience?

I have not taught there so much, but I might say that I have taught there intensively. The discovery of America is a story it would be good to know how to tell. I discovered it belatedly. I had gone to Chicago a few times at Bloom's invitation, but as for going there for a longer stay and living there a bit, I did this only belatedly. From the outset, we both wanted to work together, and they invited me and treated me both generously and as a friend—in a way for which I am not only truly grateful, but which continues to surprise me.

There is much generosity in America. It seems to me there is no other country in European history that has been in a position to play, and capable of playing, so generously this role of offering, not only a refuge to the earth's unfortunate, but also an incomparable working situation for those judged capable of putting it to good use. And the experience of the American university caused me to appreciate how mistaken is our usual idea of it.

Today in France we have this idea—and I fear, in the government itself—that the American university is based on competition. Competition is a salient element of American life, to be sure! Universities do not escape this. But this is not what is essential. What that part of French opinion that wishes to "introduce competition among universities as in the United States" does not take into account is to what point the Americans invest their pride and glory in their universities. It is a matter of honor, still more than profit.

It is often said—and it is not false—that the universities, on their campuses, are foreign bodies within American life. But it must also be recognized that they represent the ultimate fulfilment of the American *cursus honorum*.[iv] An American who becomes rich will often mark and crown this success by founding a chair or financing a research institute at a university. Indeed, it is not necessary to be rich to do this. Former students, the alumni, feel responsible for supporting their alma mater financially. I am deliberately employing the Latin terms that make up the common American vocabulary in order to emphasize that the American university has retained an attachment to classical studies that is more widespread and more lively than is the case in Europe. Many universities have "great books" or classics programs, from Homer to Proust, and the liberal arts colleges are universities that teach mathematics, philosophy, ancient languages, literature, and history over a four-year curriculum.

You have much good to say of this American university of which Bloom spoke so ill!

Bloom fought against the decline of the virtues of the American university, the relative vigor of which I have remarked. I am certainly too far away to be a good judge. Bloom was a passionate participant, and his diagnosis is very acute, but he perhaps is a bit lacking in equanimity. I do not know. In any case, the vices of "relativism" that he denounces are those of society itself; they are not proper to the university, even if it might be up to the university to brake rather than foment these vices.

My point is not to paint a uniformly splendid vision of the American university. In any case, it doesn't need my help, since everyone wants to teach or to study in the United States. I do not think, in any case, that it can serve as a model for the French university. The former has been so abundantly endowed with financial means for such a long time, while the latter has been on meager rations for so long that the plan to build American-style campuses in France is a ridiculous idea. For example, we are promised a "great campus for the social sciences," when we do not even have the research funding necessary to retain some excellent doctoral students, who must then go to look for funding in Canada or, precisely, in the United States. What I admire in the United States—you might well say that my admiration is not disinterested—is that this country invests its pride in its universities. No one would think to say that of France. This utilitarian and capitalist people invests its pride in its universities, and we, on the other hand, a people dedicated to the adventures of the mind, we despise them and let them vegetate in humiliating poverty.

Let me be clear here. What I admire in the wealth of the American universities is not the wealth itself but the political or moral significance of this wealth. I am prepared, moreover, to say that the American university is, in a way, too wealthy, that its intellectual productivity is far from proportionate to its wealth, and that I can imagine no good reason why Harvard University should have an endowment comparable to a good-sized country.

As far as I am concerned, what I found in the American university, is, of course, what strikes anyone who comes from Europe and especially France, that is, not only the extremely favorable working conditions, but something else as well that is more important and that we try with great difficulty to produce at the School, namely, this movement that meshes student life with the life of teaching in a natural way. In the French tradition, there is a gulf between teachers and students; you are a student or you are a teacher, and there is no transition. In American university life, advanced students take on teaching or tutorial functions early on while they work on their theses, such that there is a gradual process that leads naturally from the condition of the undergraduate student to that of the full professor, passing through the intermediate stages. There is this natural movement. Thus, university life brings with it its own complex sociability, which can have its problems, but which seems to me to present a major benefit for students: it *encourages* them.

IV. Teaching Political Philosophy

The teacher of political philosophy is naturally motivated to express himself in public. Is there a certain kind of public intervention appropriate to the political philosopher?

As I said at the beginning of the interview, I have always considered myself, mainly and even uniquely, as someone who is seeking to understand. My main and almost exclusive activity is certainly intellectual activity or research, and I have never been subject to the temptation or the ambition often attributed to us to change togas, as it were, from that of the teacher to that of the senator. I have always felt that intellectual work constituted a complete life, and that, in any case, I could not lead two at the same time, that I was capable of only one, and this was the intellectual life.

Obviously, when one deals with political questions one necessarily intervenes in a sense in the public square, since one advances propositions on political things. What one writes, therefore, of course has political significance, even if this does not directly concern the present political situation. When, for example, I consider Tocqueville's interpretation of democracy, which I analyze as I have analyzed it in the little book on Tocqueville, well, in a certain way, I am saying something about contemporary democracy. And when, further, I conclude by saying: "to love democracy well, one must love it moderately" (a formula, the success of which I admit, I did not anticipate), then, to be sure, I provoke certain political reactions, in the ordinary sense of the term.

I believe, nevertheless, that the two activities must really not be confused. And if, obviously, I wish that what I say—because I think that it is true rather than false—might find an echo among my fellow citizens, this is not my main preoccupation. Everyone prefers to be read than ignored, but, once again, to attain influence over public opinion, political and social influence—I may deceive myself, but I think that this is not among my primary preoccupations. I added immediately that I do not recommend staying outside the public square. It even happens that I intervene directly through interviews, statements, or articles on contemporary political subjects.

I do so for two reasons, one of which may seem to you unconvincing, while for me, it is primordial.

The reason that requires no commentary is that it certainly is part of being civil and being a citizen to give one's opinion on public questions when asked, assuming there is no impediment. This is part of good civic manners. But there is another reason, a more intellectual reason, one might say an epistemological reason, and that is that I believe that political reflection is made up of at least two things: there is, obviously, work on the great themes of political philosophy and political history, but there is also the capacity to share political experience and to participate in it. You will recall Machiavelli's formula: "the reading of ancient things, and the experience of modern things." I believe that it is absolutely imperative, in order to elaborate a serious political science, to maintain one's capacity to experience modern things open, intact, and active. Thus, in a way, by responding to a request for political commentary, by striving to interpret political developments, by analyzing a political situation or a social situation, I am exercising this capacity or, as Montaigne would say, I am "essaying" this capacity. This is a way of validating, of testing the integrity of my faculties of understanding, I would say. Otherwise, one finds oneself in this situation—I do not say that it is frequent, but it is not rare—in which one is able to elaborate a very subtle and very refined comprehension of political philosophy or of a historical situation, and yet one is without eyes or ears before the present political situation. Contrary to what is commonly believed, and this brings us back to Aron, the capacity to perceive what is happening right in front of us, to be sensitive, as Péguy said, to the bite of the present, is something rare to possess and difficult to acquire.

Intervention in public debate is thus a way to activate this faculty, to put it to the test. I have done it only rarely. I do it when I think, rightly or wrongly, that I have something to say and when the situation allows me to hope that a few might hear me. This is what I did with the little book on the nation,[v] since I proposed there some reflections on the nation at a time when it was clear that its fate had become a subject of preoccupation for many of my fellow citizens.

Was your Cours familier de philosophie politique[vi] *a different form of intervention in the city by a political philosopher?*

The *Cours familier* is based somewhat on the same epistemology. What was supposed to be covered in this course? The task was to present the great issues of the contemporary world to second-year students at *Sciences Po*.[vii] This presents a very specific difficulty, for in this case, one does not get to choose one's subject. If one is not to give an extremely partial or one-sided class, one must confront the problems that plainly manifest themselves in contemporary society, problems that necessarily and naturally concern citizens, in an intelligible way. One is thus brought to treat questions that one might not be particularly eager to take on as carefully as possible. This is not an easy exercise, but this is again an exercise that makes it possible to experience the validity of one's approach and to see whether one is able to respond in a reasonably coherent manner to the body of political problems of a given society.

Besides your students, whom are you addressing? Is it the body of citizens as a whole, the "cultivated public," or those who make political decisions? Can a true philosopher be a good adviser to the prince?

You know that I have always declined that title. I believe, in any case, that there are very few examples of true philosophers who have been the prince's counselor. This is because, in the first place, the true philosopher will not wish to get close to the prince, because, when one gets close to the prince, then one enters into a force field that makes the practice of philosophy difficult. Symmetrically, the prince will not wish for a philosopher to get close to him. Why? Because the prince wants to be prince. And if it is a true philosopher who is coming near him, his principality and his mastery will be put in question. Even if the world is ignorant that the philosopher is a philosopher and that he is paying the prince a visit, the prince will feel, in his very being, that the philosopher claims mastery over the prince, or that the philosopher cannot help exercising and experiencing his superiority in relation to the prince. And this is something the prince cannot tolerate. I would say they have incompatible souls.

What then must be done? The philosopher is an educator; he educates the civic body and tries to formulate the terms of legislation by bringing out the criteria of justice. He tries to instruct the legislator in general, and he tries to instruct the citizen in general, or to instruct those citizens who desire and are capable of a certain impartiality. Let us say that he dispenses a general teaching—as Aristotle does in his *Politics*, which is the supreme example of a book of political education—but one that does not need to be said within the prince's hearing, but is rather offered to the citizen body. This, according to me, is the only reasonable, useful, and possible intervention for the philosopher, and even for one who, without being exactly a philosopher, strives to understand public things.

PART FIVE:
THE COMMON AND THE UNIVERSAL

THE EVIDENCE OF THE UNIVERSAL, AND THE INDETERMINACY OF THE COMMON

We were speaking just now of the "Ciceronian moment." Could this notion be applied to the present political situation?

What I have called the "Ciceronian moment" is this period during which Europeans did not really know what political form, or more generally, what human association they could or they wanted to live under. The human association that had the most authority was the empire. Europeans were always trying to re-establish the empire, without any lasting political success; finally, it was another political form, the nation, that prevailed—I have already evoked the role that the Reformation played in this victorious crystallization of the national form. From this time forward and for many centuries, the nation was considered the natural frame of civilized human life. I recall that Aron liked to cite a text of Mauss's in which the nation was presented as the political form *par excellence*, the culmination of human civilization. And there is no doubt that, at the end of the 19th century and still at the beginning of the 20th, Europeans, in different nations, had the sense of inhabiting the most fully developed political form and human association.

As you know, this idea has become very foreign to us because the nation, for reasons that we will not consider here, was discredited in Europe and appeared more and more as a type of human association belonging to the past. We had also undertaken the edification of a new political form, or at least we envisioned the perspective of a new political form that we call "Europe," however this is to be conceived. We continue to belong to the old nation and we envision belonging to Europe, which already forms a part of our experience, but in a way that I find extremely limited and artificial.

This uncertain situation would be very difficult to experience and would induce much anxiety and much reflection, perhaps much disorder, if the uncertainty were not largely attenuated or covered up by the spiritual conviction that, whatever our political membership, there is something more profound, that is, our being a part of humanity (I say "spiritual" because this conviction is not linked to a political institution or experience). The uncertainty of political membership, or the gravity of this uncertainty, is veiled from our eyes because we feel we have an immediate access to humanity. Feeling that we are naturally and immediately members of humanity, we perceive political memberships as a secondary consideration. The fact that we have several political affiliations at our disposition not only does not appear to us as a problem to be resolved, but is often even presented as an advantage or a sign of the superiority of the present condition of Europeans.

You know the argument: the plurality of affiliations does not constitute a problem, since there is no reason to choose among them; the multiplicity of affiliations is, on the contrary, an abundance. Is it not a kind of abundance to be equally and at once Breton, French, European, and a citizen of the world? I believe that this presentation is seductive but deceptive. All these affiliations are in fact drawn toward or absorbed in our belonging to humanity. But humanity does not constitute a political body, since it is incapable of self-government. Certain circumstances, mainly American protection and dominance, have allowed the relaxation of political necessity in Europe, and almost allowed it to be suspended. And since they are on vacation, Europeans believe that they will never have to work. Let them enjoy it, because this will not last.

What, in your view, might be the consequences of this European vacation?

If nation states are in the process of disappearing in Europe, it is the matrix of European life that is being undone. For this reason, the scope of the recomposition that will be necessary is considerable. We will have to accomplish something radical that has very rarely been accomplished in history, that is, to found a new political form. It is time we understood this. And it is time that we prepare ourselves for the end of these great European vacations, an end that cannot be far off.

And why is this so? The religion of humanity, which is a veil over our eyes and a down comforter to our hearts, draws its credibility from political conditions it is itself incapable of creating. Europeans may think that they are natural citizens of humanity because they have no need to defend themselves, because they do not need to take responsibility for their own defense. Europe as a whole can conceive itself as the avant-garde of a pacified humanity because the United States is still taking responsibility for the defense of Europe. The European religion of humanity, then, rests ultimately on American force. Europeans are now living on the inertia of the national form, on what I called the religion of humanity, and on American protection. This does not make up a vigorous political order, or one likely to last.

Thus, it is very probable that the European area will soon be the space of powerful recompositions of common life, and we do not know what form these recompositions will take. Let us at least hope that they will be peaceful. For, to repeat, if we take the question of political forms seriously, if we gauge the importance that they have had in the history of European order and disorder, then we can assess the depth of the upheaval that will come about when the inertia that holds the European order together has run its course—when we will be obliged *effectively* to constitute a new political form capable of succeeding the nation-state. We are talking about something deeper than a revolution, because a revolution involves only a change of regime.

Obviously, one might also imagine a Europe that continues its peaceful decline demographically and politically, until it becomes a Mediterranean or an Atlantic dependency, unless it is divided between Atlantic powers and, let us say, the Mediterranean, that is, Muslim, region. Turkey's entry into the European Union would signify precisely the fulfillment of this latter possibility. But if Europe intends to continue historically, it faces the necessity, either of producing an unprecedented political form, or of giving new life to traditional elements, that is, to the old nations on the one hand and, perhaps, to the old religion on the other. In any case, there is no future for Europe in European projects as now constituted, no future for Europe in the Commission or in the Parliament, since, precisely, the projects and these institutions do not take into account the question of political form, or even the question of regime. Sooner or later, Europeans will have to remember the political condition of humanity.

Among the possible responses to Europe's current situation, you suggest giving new life to the old nations and to the old religion. Is this a realistic political proposition? To what degree are these traditional elements still available? How might one "give them new life"?

I am not making such a proposal; this is a possibility I envision. The spectrum of possibilities is not unlimited; on the contrary, it is terribly restricted. I can only manage to conceive three great possibilities. The least probable is the "heroic" production of a new political form. If you discern today in Europe a person, a country, or an institution capable of fulfilling this founding role, please tell me. A more probable outcome is that we will abandon ourselves more and more to inertia, that we will drink the last drop from the narcotic cup of moralizing. "We feel so good."[viii] But in the end external pressure—economic, political, military, migratory—from countries or regions that not only do not share our religion of humanity but that even despise it (do you believe the Chinese or the Muslims consider themselves citizens of the world?), such pressures will perhaps provoke what I would call survival reactions, something like "all the same, we do not want to die." Perhaps we will want to save at least something of European life. And so, the only thing I am saying is that, in these conditions, a third possibility, the old nations and the old religion would be an inestimable resource—if only because we have no other. How to give them new life? I do not know, but necessity, as Machiavelli taught us, is a great teacher.

V. The Common and the Universal

Is the contemporary religion of humanity based on faith in philosophical ideas? Do we not tend to confuse our democratic city with the city of philosophy?

Indeed. Contemporary Europeans feel that they are living a philosophical fulfillment. If they no longer believe in their civilizing mission, in the white man's burden, they remain persuaded that they are the avant-garde of humanity: humanitarian colonizers, de-colonizers, and post-colonizers, we are always the first according to our judgment. Today, we are showing the world what peace and democracy will be at the end of history, and we offer our peace to the rest of the world to imitate. We are showing our less advanced brethren how the human adventure culminates. This conviction, which is so powerful among Europeans, results from several factors that are hard to unravel.

One of the main ones certainly has to do with what you were saying, that is, with the hold of philosophy or of certain philosophical ideas on the European mind since the 18th century. It is in the 18th century, I believe, that the reference of humanity became entirely detached from any human association, even the largest and vastest empire, even the most universal Church. Nothing like this had ever happened before. Up until this time, the great political strategies of universality had produced either imperial or ecclesiastical political projects—Alexander's empire, the Roman Empire, the Catholic Church. The universal, up to this point, had always been a universal empire, even when it was based on philosophy, when it was understood as the realization of philosophy. After all, the idea of a philosophic empire is very old: this is the interpretation that Plutarch already gave to Alexander's empire, and that Dante will later give to the Holy Roman Empire. For Plutarch as for Dante, Alexander's empire or the Holy Roman Empire are the fulfillment of Aristotle's philosophy. And reciprocally, for them, Aristotle's philosophy is fulfilled in the political form of the empire.

On the other hand, the humanity that we have celebrated since the 18th century is neither a Church, nor an empire, but an idea that envelops all human associations, and whose authority prevails over all human associations, even the most vast empire, even the most universal Church. This idea that emerges in the 18th century did not have the time to complete its career during that century, since, beginning with the French Revolution, this notion of humanity, which the Enlightenment understood in opposition to the Church as vaster and "more humane" than the Church, will be mediated by the nation—mediated, that is to say, made concrete and real, but also, of course, limited and circumscribed.

Unlike "humanity," which is in principle one, nations are plural, and European nations are rivals, and will increasingly be rivals, each one claiming to make real and concrete the most noble, complete, and satisfying humanity. This history, which here I am recalling so briefly, is that of the 19th and early 20th centuries. But today European nations have lost much of their legitimacy in two world wars, and the notion of humanity elaborated in the 18th century is re-appearing in its original philosophical self-evidence; it re-appears not only without any felt need for mediation, but accompanied by a vigilant hostility regarding all mediation and all concretization. Whoever evokes the need for a mediation to render humanity concrete—the mediation of a nation or of any other political form—is immediately suspected of being, if not an enemy of humanity, at least a too lukewarm friend. Anyone who does not see humanity as an immediate reality, as an evident experience in a way, reveals, according to the dominant opinion, his hostility to human unity and thus to humanity itself. Such is the authority among us of this idea, or philosophic origin, of humanity.

The many phenomena included in the notion of globalization support this philosophical idea, don't they?

Precisely—what real, observable phenomena are covered by the notion of globalization? But first: what do we even mean by this notion? It is the occasion and the means of much confusion. In a word, there is a general tendency to confuse problems related to communication and homogenization on the one hand, and what might contribute to a true unification of the world on the other.

But the phenomena of the first kind are in no way factors in the second: six or seven billion human beings wearing Nike shoes, speaking English and exchanging messages on the internet make for a homogeneous world, but not necessarily one that is unified. What is important are the opinions and passions that motivate human beings, and where these are concerned, there is nothing to suggest that we are getting closer to a unified world.

Europeans believe, or pretend to believe, that other large groups of human beings obey the same motives as themselves or, to be more precise, the motives that have motivated them only *very recently*. But this is not true. The large national or religious associations of the non-Western world are involved in a process in which their power is rising, and they embrace this process as such. This is as true of Brazil as it is of China or of the Muslim world. This may announce a more equal or "multilateral" world, but certainly not a more unified world; whatever unity the world has enjoyed up to this point has been based on Western dominance. Every great process of globalization has been one of Westernization. Now we are seeing the warning symptoms of what might be called the de-Westernization of the world.

In Europe itself, there is neither true unification nor even real homogenization. In particular, a part of the new generation of the Muslim population tends to live in social and spiritual autarky, and this contributes to a fragmentation, indeed, a dislocation of European sociability. As you know, we are not supposed to mention or even to *see* all these phenomena. The official European doctrine, or the official philosophy of Europe (for there is one), does not leave us free to see what we see.

According to this public philosophy, we see, we must see, we can only see human unity, or at least humanity in the process of unification. But if we claim to see what we do not see, if what is visible and what is visibly fragmented do not arrest our gaze, and if, on the contrary, we believe we are seeing the invisible unity of humanity, then we are indeed part of what we can only call a religion, part of what I am happy to call, following others, the religion of humanity. We are not only under the power of an idea; rather, the philosophical idea of humanity comes along with a religious enthusiasm. Obviously, as always in such circumstances, those who do not share this enthusiasm are exposed to the sacred indignation of those who are prey to it. To force someone to believe what he does not see—is this not a definition of fanaticism, and particularly of religious fanaticism?

If democracy in Europe, supported by the philosophical idea of humanity, has become the object of a religion, then what remains of the questioning that underlies our regime?

According to the evidence, our democracy is no longer capable of welcoming or of raising questions, and first and foremost, questions relating to political philosophy, questions that we know well such as: "What is it to be just?" or "What are the criteria of justice?" Our democracy answers before the question can be posed; the question must not be raised, the question of the best regime must not be raised, since we are dealing with something self-evident, a self-evidence that is one with the feeling of humanity itself. Anyone who today pursues the questions of political philosophy, who examines the criteria of the best regime, must be someone who does not feel the evident goodness of democracy with sufficient intensity. Anyone who raises such questions will be interrogated by democracy, by the democratic vigilance that this religion evokes. Rather than democracy appearing before the tribunal of reason, like everything else, it is reason, particularly questioning reason, that is, political philosophy, that appears before the tribunal of the religion of humanity. This, I believe, is our situation, a situation in which political reflection is reduced to what is called democratic theory.

What is democratic theory? It is an axiomatic system that starts with the unquestioned truth of the principles of modern democracy and unfolds its consequences, which are, of course, variable according to the ingeniousness of the authors in question—but the amplitude of the variations is very small. Today, in the universities, the theory of democracy is an immense machine for producing more of the same, the same theoretical fabric for covering up the intellectual life of our departments of political science with an "ashen snowfall," to borrow Charles Péguy's formula. Academics and researchers are thus chosen for their capacity to say, more ingeniously than the rest, the same things as everyone else. And so it has been for more than thirty years, in which half (and this is hardly an exaggeration) of all works in political theory consist in commenting endlessly on the work of John Rawls (*A Theory of Justice* and other works), which is certainly a very respectable body of work, but one that is all the same limited and, in any case, entirely subjected to the prejudices of the era that John Rawls confines himself to making explicit with great care. I am inclined to say that no tyrant, with the help of all his henchman, would have been able to achieve such monotony.

Would you compare this situation of political philosophy to a new form of the end of philosophy, following those envisioned by Marx and Heidegger.

The situation is, in effect, very difficult for philosophy. When it is the very notions that philosophy has elaborated that return to it as ideas that can no longer be questioned, then one can say that philosophy has become the slave of its creations. Philosophy, in its first movement, emerges by distinguishing itself from particular notions, from particular concretizations of what is human, from particular customs, ways of life and religions, in order to set forth a human universal, of course, with a certain degree of variation in the way this human universal is understood by philosophers. And it is true that, in the contemporary situation, since the universal that philosophy once aimed at has become a common and obligatory opinion imposed by social authority, it is the very idea of humanity that prevents us from questioning humanity.

Under these conditions, philosophy, and especially political philosophy, has great difficulty surviving, since, precisely, it is what it has discovered that now prevents its activity—hence the weakening, the thinning-out of political philosophy, in fact, its near-disappearance in the period that has seen the unmediated triumph of the modern notion of humanity. I do not mean to suggest that, in the domain of political philosophy as in others, all resistance to the empire of the same is concentrated in the "village of the Gauls," but it is true that, today, there are not many of us! We look down on centuries that we would call less civilized than our own, in the sense that intellectual development was less widespread, that philosophy was not yet popular, but in fact those centuries were more favorable to philosophy. And since you have cited Marx, I do not know whether what Marx called "the world's becoming philosophical" has been good for the world, but there is no doubt that it has not been good for philosophy.

This idea of humanity as opposed to political mediations delegitimizes all efforts to reconstitute a common good, something held in common. Can you define this notion of "common" that is becoming so foreign to us?

As it emerges among the Greeks, the notion of the common is an active notion. There is a Greek verb for this, that is, *koinônein*, which can be translated as "having or putting in common." Therefore, when I speak of "the common," I am speaking of "putting in common;" this is an operation that is never finished and that cannot be fully possessed.

There are signs or expressions of the common: there is a public place; there are public buildings and a place, the assembly, but the common thing is an operation that the citizens carry out, with more or less success to be sure. The common is a task; it is purpose; it is the production of an order in which human beings can conduct their lives in the most deliberate way possible.

What is most often striking is the degree to which the common is badly served, or badly produced, or devoured by the particular. The common is a notion that was of course ignored by civilizations of the family or of the familial order, but it also risks being lost from sight when the springs of the civic order are weakened. To be sure, the moderns are not ignorant of the quest for the common, but this quest encounters a specific difficulty in our individualist civilizations. This is because we suppose that the individual already disposes of human rights, that he already possesses them: we understand the individual as one whose rights are given: man is the being who has rights. And since the rights of the individual are attached to a tangible individual, these rights seem to be more self-evident than the common, which never exists, properly speaking, as an object which can never be touched. We can touch an individual, but we cannot touch what is common. The notion of the individual seems clear; the notion of the common seems vague. The philosophy of what is common is condemned to struggle against this epistemological bias of contemporary democratic civilization.

If we take the great disciplines of contemporary society—law and economics—we see that they are based, respectively, on rights and on individual interests, and that they presuppose the disappearance of the common. Certainly they show no concern for what is common. Economics postulates that each individual follows his interests; contemporary law is based on individual, subjective rights. There is no recognized discipline that takes responsibility for what is common, and this is thus vulnerable to being relegated to the realm of vague ideas, ideological abstractions or the imagination. It seems to me all the more necessary to develop a way of speaking of what is common, whether this is called political science or political philosophy.

Might one say that we have moved from the "common" in the active sense as understood by the Greeks to "common" in the passive sense of "common denominator."

Since we are engaged in a process of depoliticization, our perspective no longer embraces common things, but in effect is based more—this is one way of putting it—on one or more common denominators, or on what is called "the general," as in, the general rule, the rule that applies to everyone. But the general rule is not the common.

The European ideal today, the ideal of European life, is that we would all be governed by general rules and that all action would be subsumed under a rule, with evaluating institutions for verifying that things are done by the rules. This, obviously, is what we call "governance." But there are no two more opposite ideas for the organization of collective life than the now dominant idea of governance by rules and the idea of the common that was, up until a quite recent time, the European and Western understanding of political life. There, I believe we see a loss of intellectual imagination. We no longer know what it means to act. We have lost the sense of action, and we understand action only as the application of the rule, or conformity to the rule. Even if we otherwise reject all divine and human laws, we understand action as conformity to the rule and not as an entry or an access into a new, properly human element, that is, the common, as participation in what is common. Of course, this idea of action as conformity to a rule has behind it all the people and all the institutions that feel called to set the rules and to verify conformity to rules. This constitutes an enormous social power in favor of this understanding of action. And a tyranny of rules is being consolidated in support of this enormous social power.

Today it is thought that the problem of the individual as belonging to the collectivity will be solved by other means than what is common. Are not the politics of recognition and of identity particularly significant in this respect?

Certainly. All recent political developments result finally from the abandonment of the perspective of the common. We are looking for a kind of politics entirely detached from any reference to what is common—a politics that is, in this sense, altogether detached from what is most fundamental to political life. This is what unfolds as, or is formulated as, the politics of recognition or politics of identity, because recognition or identity designate what the members of society already are, what they are by their ethnic origin, what they are by their sex, or what they are by their sexual orientation, as we say today.

V. The Common and the Universal

The politics of recognition or of identity undertakes to make this characteristic visible by granting them the blessing of the public space. This is still a form of politics to the degree that reference is made to the public space and that something is brought into public view, but it is a politics whose goals or consequence is to leave things *as they are*: these human beings, these members of society, have a certain identity and this is the identity that is to be recognized. What is entirely lost is the idea that the political order consists, for human beings of different identities, in *producing* something in common, in producing something that *did not heretofore exist*. All this presupposes, to repeat, that there cannot be something in common, and since there can be nothing in common, the task of politics is to meet each individual in his or her particularity in order to bring this particularity into the light of the public space. This is the new meaning of politics. It is clear that this is a perspective that tends to deprive the political order of what is essential to it. We can still say that there is a public space, a public light, but certainly not something common, since, to repeat, particularities alone are seen as truly real.

I would like to bring out the social and moral danger of the loss of the common through the example of an actual phenomenon that is very curious. Let us return to the question of equality. We are very ambitious regarding this question of equality because each of us, each individual, is addressed by a double imperative. On the one hand, we are subject to the egalitarian imperative, linked with the feeling of sameness of which we were speaking: one must be compassionate, recognize the other as oneself, that is, as equal as possible; we must see every person as the same as ourselves. But, on the other hand, there is estrangement; the individual is subject to the opposite injunction, which is to be as unequal as possible, that is, to be as competitive as possible in order to show his competence, success, and contribution to the value added to society in terms of the received economic and social indicators.

It seems to me that, for the self-constitution of the subject, as we say today, and for the situating of the individual within social life, this double injunction creates a very uncomfortable situation.

This oscillation between these two opposite perspectives belongs, in a sense, to the human being as a social being, but it is made more extreme and harder to control by the fact, precisely, that the disposition of the common, the public space, does not contain the orienting elements that would allow the individual to find his place somewhat in his relation to the collectivity, to relate to something like a "measure." The disappearance, or at least the fading of "social circles" and "classes," which constitutes the *cool*[ix] charm of our fine contemporary society, means, at the same time, the loss of orienting elements that once tended to prevent the agent from doing "whatever." When anyone (no matter who) is the equal and the rival to anyone else (no matter whom), then, it's no matter what—*anything goes.*[x]

So the common might be a guide and a stabilizing factor for the wandering contemporary individual, who slips from one extreme to another?

In fact, in the civic order, what is common addresses two calls, two demands or two injunctions to the members of society; above all, it in a way determines a point of perspective for each individual—to each his own tastes, talents, and other characteristics, but finally, it is what is common that calls, and each individual relates to what is common, or to one or another version, or section, of what is common. I am not talking about the "moral law," but simply about those collective "expectations" that the member of society normally feels he should satisfy, in varying degrees, of course. For example, the acquisitive instinct is moderated, not by the moral law or by the Gospel's teaching, but by taking into account "what is done" in "our social circles." So when I speak of one's relation to what is common, I refer to a very vast array of phenomena, which go from simple social conformism to heroic devotion to the city.

The way things are now, on the contrary, where the relation to what is common is fading away (whether what is common is the school, the business, or the republic), and where we oscillate between being as equal and being as unequal as possible, we fall back into a kind of state of nature, a state of nature in which we never know what will be our relation to whomever we meet. Will we meet one like ourselves, and so make peace and work in harmony? Or will we forget our sameness and consider that we are in a situation of competition and of war, and thus that it is natural to make war and "put the pressure on"? In this sense there is something very demoralizing about contemporary society because we are ceaselessly driven from one disposition to the other, and these two opposite dispositions cannot be part of a good mixture in which each moderates the other. Hence, the bad mixture of sentimental humanitarianism and unchained competition that characterizes our society and which, I believe, is linked to this loss of relation to what is common. Have you noticed that some of our most competitive contemporaries come precisely from the "humanitarian" sphere?

The point is not to imagine some idyllic earlier condition in which common things oriented each person's life in some harmonious fashion. What was common could be heavy, even oppressive. But we are talking about present-day society, and in this society, it is the fading of what is common whose consequences are unfolding. If one has nothing like a common perspective that is authoritative for the members of society—with all the inevitable attendant difficulties and uncertainties, but at least something authoritative—then one is ceaselessly falling back into this oscillation between compassionate identification and competitive ferocity. There is truly something here that is a matter of political epistemology: we cannot manage to perceive, to feel what is common. It is not that people have become bad citizens; rather, spontaneously and sincerely they are able to see as real only what is attached directly to an individual. Identity, recognition, compassion, and competition; all these notions have to do only with individuals or with relations among individuals.

In the end, what is happening in our time is a profound transformation of the collective imagination. After all, the constitution of the nations presupposed a reconfiguration of the collective imagination in order for members of society finally to be able to persuade themselves that they were members of the same community:

for an inhabitant of Brest and one of Perpignan to feel that they belong to the same community requires an effort and requires a certain disposition of the imagination. And now it seems that the "community-making" imagination (I don't dare say "communing"), the imagination that bears what is common, is weakened, that it is no longer active, that it doubts itself radically.

CHRISTIANITY AND DEMOCRACY

To return to the egalitarian pole of the contemporary double injunction: in your view does the religion of the semblable (*the one who is the same*) *find its source in the religion of the neighbor?*

The religion of humanity, the religion of the same, would certainly not have attained its empire over our souls if it did not appear as the extension and the consequence, perhaps the effectual truth, of Christianity, of the religion of the neighbor. And I believe it is right to say that the feeling of the same appears to us as the modern form, thus the truly human form, the final human form of Christian charity.

This is quite a difficult question to unravel. It is true that the feeling that goes with democracy, compassion, often gives rise to the same actions that charity produces. Nevertheless, the perspective is radically different. The feeling of sameness is an ingenious adjustment of self-love. Since I perceive him as like me, I identify with a fellow-sufferer, and thus I desire to deliver him from his suffering, just as I would desire to be delivered from my own. At the same time, of course, compassion presupposes that I am not myself suffering. My moral imagination must be, so to speak, at its leisure; it must have some play in it in order to be able to apply itself to another's suffering. If I am myself suffering, at least with a certain intensity, I lose this availability. And as Rousseau, to whom we owe the most rigorous analyses of humanitarian compassion, emphasizes, the most sincere compassion always carries with it, along with the identification with the suffering other, the satisfaction and pleasure of not suffering oneself.

Charity is altogether different. In the strict or full sense of the term, it is a disposition, a virtue that man cannot acquire or produce by his own strength. Technically, if I can put it this way, charity is the love of God, the love by which God loves mankind and, first of all, the love by which God loves himself in the Trinitarian communion. Thus, in the proper sense of the term, something is charitable if it partakes, by God's grace, in God's love. This is a theological definition, and in this context we can set it aside. But even if we look at this disposition from a simply human perspective, we see that charity takes on certain traits that distance it from democratic compassion. In effect, charity has nothing to do with the return to the self that belongs to the very life of the feeling of sameness because charity involves neither identification with the suffering other nor the satisfied and pleasant feeling of not suffering oneself.

In charity, there is neither identification with the other, nor return to the self, quite simply because charity frees us from the human plane of things and from this double and unique slavery to the other and to oneself. In this sense, charity delivers us from compassion. In charity, the one who is loved is loved—to use an expression that says so much—for the love of God; he is loved as the image of God. And this is for a quite simple reason: in the Christian perspective, only God is truly loveable, thus the human being is only loveable because he is in the image of God. Thus, one who loves from charity leaves himself and does not return, and, in the other sense, he tends to remove his self from the one he loves, since he sees him as an image of God and loves him for the love of God. He does not love him because he is the same as himself (the lover), and he does not love him because he is this particular person; he loves him because he is the image of God. And who is the image of God? Every person, when he is seen according to charity. This is why one who is loved from charity is designated so modestly and, as it were, so flatly as the "neighbor"; he is neither "the same" nor "the other person," which are two names that we give to someone whom we are not. The neighbor is neither the same, nor the other; he requires no subtle phenomenology of the same and the other. He is the one whom one meets. "And who is my neighbor," asked the lawyer—you recall Luke's Gospel. But on the road that goes down from Jerusalem to Jericho, the Samaritan has no difficulty recognizing his neighbor.

Does Christian action on behalf of the most disadvantaged arise from humanitarianism or from charity?

Today, in the West, the religion of the neighbor and the religion of the same tend to be mixed and confused. It is truly difficult to make the difference we are speaking of even somewhat comprehensible to public opinion. Since the sign of charity is effective service to the neighbor, and since humanitarianism accomplishes effective service to the neighbor, or rather, in the event, to others like oneself, humanitarianism seems to fulfill Christianity. The distinctive perspective of Christianity is lost to view. Abbé Pierre (I speak of his public persona, not of his soul) represented very well, it seems to me, this point at which Christian charity tends to lose itself almost entirely in the democratic religion of the same. God was entirely absent from his public statements. On the other hand, even though Mother Teresa displayed her heroic virtues in humanitarian service, she did it from a perspective that opens on specifically Christian dimensions not found within humanitarianism. Without judging persons, Abbé Pierre and Mother Teresa seem to me, in a way, to be opposite figures. One puts us in confusion and the other helps us to get out of it.

You were speaking of notions that philosophy has discovered and that now prevent it, paradoxically, from going forward. Do we not see a similar phenomenon in Christianity, which discovered the "neighbor" and now does not know what to think of democratic sameness?

Yes, this is a judicious comparison. It is true that it is Christianity itself that brought about this difficulty, since it takes on the task of judging based on charity, and charity is obliged to judge by the effects of charity, and the effects of charity are evident in the service of the neighbor, which looks very much like humanitarian aid. The difference is that the service of the neighbor—I return to what I was just saying—is not carried out from the same perspective by Mother Teresa and by a humanitarian doctor. In a word, humanitarian compassion or the feeling of sameness focuses mainly on the body; Christian charity focuses on souls and concerns itself with bodies to the degree that the fate of souls is in part linked with the condition of bodies. Mother Teresa never imagined that her function, or rather her vocation, consisted simply in caring for or nourishing the body, but in acting for the salvation of the unfortunate. Obviously, if the Christian perspective has become obscure or even entirely lost, if the notion of "salvation of the soul" has become unintelligible, then the difference between charity and humanitarian compassion is also lost.

All this is very difficult for public opinion to sort out because it is all involved in vast confusions that affect the very self-understanding of our democracies. Part of the problem, as I was saying, is that our democracies understand themselves as the realization of Christianity or of what is best, what is "most human" in Christianity. In this sense, the confusion of the two dispositions or two virtues, charity and compassion, goes to the heart of contemporary democracy. This is a mistake and a confusion, but it is constitutive of the public feeling that characterizes our societies.

To go deeper into this question of the relationship between Christianity and democracy, how would you describe the link between Christianity and equality?

This question of the relationship between Christianity and democracy is worth considering in its full implications. Here, again, is a question that is difficult to sort out, and we are lost if we begin, as is often done, in terms of "values." In my history textbook for the final year of *lycée*, as I recall vividly, it was explained that the West combined Greek and Roman values with Christian values and the values of the Enlightenment. If this is meant to remind us that paganism, Christianity, and the democratic revolution are the three great stages of Western development, then that is fine. But beyond that, this piling up of values offers no clarity.

The confusion surrounding the relationship between Christianity and democracy stems, I think, largely from the very approximative usage we make of the notion of equality. Good minds, even sometimes excellent minds (since Tocqueville is included), suggest or affirm that the root or the ultimate source of democratic equality is in the teaching of Jesus. Very well. The Gospels are open to everyone; they can be read by everyone. For my part, I have never yet found anything in the Gospels that resembles democratic equality or the principles of the philosophy of human rights.

One generally adds that democratic equality is "secularized" Christian equality. And, in fact, the theory of secularization is maintained or held to be plausible particularly on the subject of equality. Now, to say that democratic equality is secularized Christian equality is to affirm a proposition that is logically inconsistent or incoherent: it self-destructs. This is because, where this question is concerned, we do not have a notion endowed with a definite content that could be applied to two different domains, that is, the other world and this one. We do not have such a notion because the very meaning of Christian equality resides in God and relates to the other world, and the very meaning of democratic equality relates to this world! Thus, the very content of equality, the very meaning of equality, depends on its application, either to the other world or to this one. There is no self-identical idea that could be applied in two different domains; we have two radically different ideas. And no imaginable transformation can account for a passage from one to the other, since they are intrinsically tied to incompatible directions of the soul. To secularize a Christian idea is obviously to destroy it insofar as it is Christian. For anyone who takes these notions seriously, there can be no intrinsic link between the democratic idea of equality and the Christian idea of equality.

V. The Common and the Universal

But do we not see some trace of a link between the two regimes of equality in history as in the history of political ideas?

On this question, history or historical experience confirms logic. It is impossible to observe a significant correlation between the progress of Christian teaching and the progress of equality, except on two precise points, to which I will return. We can say that, in a very general way, the centuries we call Christian accommodated themselves very well to immense differences of rank and of fortune. And while Christian teaching preached charity and mildness to the mighty of this world, it also preached docility and obedience to the weak and to the poor. The most cited and commented proposition of St. Paul, and the one that has probably had the most social and political effects, was this: "Obey the powers that be!" It was only when an explicitly and even aggressively anti-Christian philosophy began to prevail in Europe that a perspective favorable to the equalizing of conditions in this world opened up. More precisely, the project of the "relief of the human condition," according to Francis Bacon's expression, then the "continuous improvement of the human condition," according to the expression of Adam Smith— these projects require at the outset, or as a precondition, the radical rejection of the Christian perspective, according to which our sickly condition can only be healed by the grace of Christ.

Consequently, if we want to attain any clarity on these questions by keeping firmly in view what is most essential to Christianity, then we must renounce these truly magical theories that claim to find the source of the modern democratic project for the improvement of the world in Christian disdain for the world.

I return to the two points that constitute exceptions to this general diagnosis. The first point is the following: though Christianity does not demand the abolition of slavery, from the beginning, it undermines the spirit of pagan warfare, which was a great supplier of slaves. In principle, it puts an end to the "*vae vitis!*," to the "woe unto the vanquished!," in the name of which the pagan victor honored his victory, one can say, by massacring the men and by reducing the women and children to slavery.

In the pagan world, there was an awful difference in condition between the conqueror and the conquered. Slavery, moreover, in its most specific quality, was tied to this difference of condition. In a way, it expressed this difference; it was its consequence and its manifestation. Now, with the irruption of Christianity, of course, war and massacres linked with war do not disappear, but this difference of condition between the conqueror and the conquered is attenuated because it is the common condition of the creature, who is a slave to sin, that is paramount. Again, Christianity does not visibly transform human conduct; men in general do not become better, or in any case, visibly better. Still, on this point, there is a profound spiritual transformation: this difference of condition, that was essential for the pagan world, is henceforth attenuated because it is enveloped in the new definition of the human condition, the condition of the creature, the condition of the sinner, of the slave to sin. This is precisely that for which Machiavelli *reproaches* Christianity: that is, for having diminished the misfortune associated with the condition of the conquered, for having decisively weakened the desire to conquer, which is the spring of a truly free political life.

There is another area in which Christianity implies the radical rejection of an inequality that was inherent in paganism. Curiously, this point is most often forgotten by the theorists of secularization. This is the matter of inequality in access to truth. For the Ancients, the most radical difference and, moreover, the most interesting difference among human beings concerns their capacity to access truth. For them, the many, who are motivated mainly by passions and by the imagination, are at best capable of acquiring right opinion if properly educated in a good regime, but are naturally incapable by themselves of obeying reason. Only the few and, ultimately, only the very few philosophers have the resources, the "natural," as Plato says, that allow them to leave behind opinions in order to attain a stable vision of what truly *is* and to conduct their lives according to this vision of what *is*—according to a "theoretical" vision. Thus, for the Ancients, the ultimate inequality, or the ultimate basis of differences among human beings, lies in the immense distance that separates the few wise from the immense crowd of those who are not wise.

Christianity, for its part, puts an end to this inequality. The truth that Christianity proposes is the same, absolutely the same, for the shepherd and the theologian. And, as you know, while the Christian religion, due to its dogmatic complexity, needs learned theologians, it has always shown a definite partiality toward shepherds and children, because they are more likely than the powerful and the learned to be "humble of heart." Thus, while Christianity has really done very little to reduce social or political inequalities (this was not and cannot be its purpose), it has, as much as it could, brought an end to the very radical separation that the Ancients imposed between the wise and everyone else. It is this, moreover, for which modern philosophers like Nietzsche will reproach Christianity, that is, precisely for having covered up or obscured, for having denied or subverted, the differences represented by the different "types" of human beings.

This, then, is what I believe can be said briefly on the subject of Christianity and democratic equality. To recapitulate: the hypothesis of a democratic secularization of Christian equality cannot be maintained, since the two ideas of equality are, as it were, unrelated; but there are two points concerning which Christianity, in effect, introduces a radical innovation in relation to paganism: on the one hand, the question of the difference between the conqueror and the conquered—here, Christianity puts an end to or goes against the cry that perhaps best expressed what was deepest in pagan life: "woe unto the vanquished!" On the other hand, there is the question of the difference between the wise and everyone else: Christianity does not recognize, or, in any case, does not recognize as a source of truth, the difference between the wise and the unwise. It is in this sense that, truly, it is "no respecter of persons."

To complete the picture, to what degree is modern freedom derived from Christianity?

It seems to me that the relationship of Christianity to freedom is more interesting and more decisive than its relationship to equality, because the notion of freedom is more humanly interesting, more meaningful than the notion of equality.

There is a Christian freedom, a specifically Christian notion of freedom, and, in a certain sense, Christianity is, of all religious or philosophical doctrines, that which attaches the most importance to freedom or to human free will. One might even say that the notion of free will is, at bottom, a Christian notion. This is a notion that applies to human nature considered in itself and independently of any eventual relation to God, but the idea of free will was only really developed in all its dimensions in the Christian context. It is not recognizable as such in ancient philosophy, nor even in most of modern philosophy.

For Christianity, as you know, the salvation of each individual plays out in acts of his or her freedom, in the way that he or she responds or does not respond to what, in pious language, we refer to as "the solicitations of grace." The simple idea is that each soul has a history proper to itself, for this history is made up of the series of free responses that each individual addresses to the divine initiative. Thus, each human soul is the protagonist and the site of a drama, in the etymological sense of the term, a drama more decisive than the most terrible political crisis or military ordeal. This is because it is a drama that is, in a way, definitive, one whose consequences are eternal. "The spiritual combat is as brutal as the battle among men," Rimbaud said—just as brutal and still more decisive, from the Christian perspective.

What holds open, so to speak, this interior space is something here again that is specific to Christianity, something that was discovered or invented by Christianity, namely, the conscience. In Christianity, freedom is tied essentially to the Christian notion of conscience. Conscience is an internal capacity of judgment, an internal tribunal that allows each human being whose conscience is awakened to be properly instructed to judge for himself as God would judge—God who, according to Augustine's expression, is "more intimate to each person than himself." God alone knows "what is in man," but each human being knows enough, through his conscience, to judge for himself in accordance with God's judgment. The Greeks had a marvelous understanding of the movements of our soul, but they knew nothing of the conscience.

Contrary to a common opinion, Sophocles' Antigone is not moved by her conscience; she is moved by an unwritten but very explicit law, namely, the law of the family. It seems to me that there is no firmer notion of human freedom, no surer resource for human freedom, than this Christian notion of conscience.

At the same time, however, the tribunal of conscience is, obviously, invisible. And this is at bottom why it was ignored by the Greeks, for whom everything that is interesting or truly significant is essentially *visible*. One might say that the Greeks have eyes, that they have only eyes; the voice of conscience is something one listens to—when one listens. Conscience is invisible; it opens up an invisible domain, but political life takes place in the visible world, and Christianity has nothing pertinent or specific to say concerning political life.

From this point of view, the air-tightness that you describe between the two regimes of equality holds true as well for the two regimes of freedom. The political consequences of the liberating notion of conscience are weak.

No doubt they are weak; they are, in any case, indirect. What I said about equality counts as well for freedom, which is the source of political life whether ancient or modern. I think it is true to say that Christianity shows little interest in political freedom. One would even have to say, more precisely, that it shows mistrust toward political freedom. Why is this? Because in political life, that is to say, in free political life, the human being invests his energies in this world and puts his confidence—sometimes an excessive confidence—in his own strength. This is political life; this is political freedom: citizens have confidence in their own strength; they are the authors of their actions. Such is the grandeur and such is the risk of political freedom. And Christianity is more alert to the risks than it is sensitive to the grandeur of political freedom. Consequently, Christianity, that is, the Christian churches, and, in particular, the Catholic Church, have tended to castigate rather than to encourage the pride of citizens.

Of course, the point of Christianity is not to order the cities of this world, but to build the city of God; this much is clear. In this sense, it is pointless to judge it according to criteria that it does not recognize. Christianity did not come to bring political freedom to the world. In a way, the criterion of political freedom is of no concern to it. Nevertheless, I think that it is legitimate to criticize it when its action on behalf of the other world, or directed toward the other world, brings about effects in this world that spoil the very humanity that it intends to perfect and lead to salvation. I am thus inclined to say that that for which I blame Christianity, or in any case the Catholic Church, is its excessive mistrust and sometimes plain enmity where manifestations of human pride are concerned, that is to say, in the modern period, where liberal and national movements are concerned. Or I might say, adversely or symmetrically, that what I hold against the Church is the preference it has too often shown toward authoritarian regimes which, as Aristotle said of tyrants, do not tolerate virile virtues in citizens.

Here, I will be blamed for rendering hasty judgment on a very complicated history. It is true that the democratic movement of modern times was accompanied by theoretical presuppositions or preambles that the Church could only condemn, as it did from the 19th to the beginning of the 20th century. The philosophy of the rights of man is, in effect, very problematic from a Christian point of view, because it in a way postulates that man gives birth to himself. The philosophy of the rights of man derives the rule of human life from man's simple humanity and not from his final purpose in God; this is the object of the church's reproach. Before this, God revealed his word and his law to man by the mediation of the Church, and now here is man declaring his own rights! The Church thus had good reason to show distrust toward the philosophy that accompanied, and that in part gave rise to, the modern democratic movement. But this source of pride and of ambition, of confidence in one's own strength, in short, this confidence in the Creation was, despite all the attendant risks, at least as worthy of encouragement by the church, it seems to me, as were the burdensome artifices of "corporate and Christian states," which, in the name of humility, bound up citizens in submission.

Here, I am speaking mainly of the Catholic Church. The same reproach could be addressed, perhaps with even more justification, to Lutheran Churches. On the contrary, Calvinism, as you know, is linked with modern freedom and with confidence in one's own strength. What are the roots of this alliance? This is a big question. I will not resolve it in a few sentences. You already know what I consider the decisive factor in the Reformation, that is, the end of ecclesiastical mediation. We have already spoken of this. I will simply add this: the conscientious soul at this time puts an end to this very instructive and salutary, but often frustrating and sometimes demoralizing conversation that it had had over such a long period with the Church that governed it. It is in the secular community that it will henceforth act and exercise judgment, thus giving this community a more penetrating religious coloration than in the old Catholic communion. Because of this withdrawal in relation to the Church, the Calvinist community brings together sensibilities whose conjunction provides the basis of the magnificent contribution of Calvinism to modern political freedom: on the one hand, there is confidence in its own strength; on the other, there is respect—a respect that is, in some ways, almost superstitious—for the law. Human power is liberated or encouraged, but no human being, religious or secular, is above the law.

WHAT IS THE WEST?

Reading you, listening to you, it seems that European history is shaped pervasively by the idea of humanity, the idea of a human universal whose definition varies according to the means of mediation. To what degree does this ceaseless quest for the universal constitute an appropriate guiding thread by which we can grasp what is distinctive about the West?

The question you raise is legitimate, even necessary, but at the same time you are leading me into a trap! As I was saying a moment ago, the religion of humanity, which is the contemporary religion of Europe and of the West, forbids us from distinguishing seriously among groups of human beings. The "right to be different" means only the prohibition from *seeing* differences. You are inviting me not only to infringe upon but to flout the Rule. I shall do it, not for the pleasure of transgression, nor even in order to persuade you in a few words of the truth of what I have proposed, but in order at least to suggest that there are questions here that are worthy of examination.

I believe, then, that there is something specific to Europe and the West, and this something embraces a certain superiority: our civilization's exploration of human possibilities is more complete than in other civilizations. But I add this immediately: on the one hand, this advantage (which, in any case, is never a given but must always be re-conquered in order not to be lost) obviously does not exempt us from the vices, defects, and weaknesses associated with the human condition; on the other hand—and this is what is most interesting—the superiority that I claim, and upon which I will explain myself in a moment, exposes us to particular *risks* to which other civilizations are not exposed or are less exposed.

What, then, is the distinguishing characteristic of the West? I would say something like this: whereas other civilizations find support in a determinate rule to which they normally recur with no urgency, Europe, or the West, has taken up a task which is at once indeterminate and urgent. Indeterminate does not here mean vague or uncertain, but rather, opened up toward a future that depends upon us. It is no longer a matter of following customs, or the law of ancestors, but of producing *something in common* [*la chose commune*]. The urgency stems from the fact that this something in common does not exist except insofar as it is produced: it is always in danger of coming undone or even being lost, hence, the opening up of a prodigiously inventive history, in particular, the incandescent arc that runs through the Greek *polis*, Athens in particular. This arc is duplicated in a second arc that we call, precisely, the West.

The question concerning justice in the common world is necessarily, at the same time, a question concerning the truth of mankind, concerning his "nature" or his "essence." That is why it is possible to say, as you suggest, that the source of Western history is—here I go!—the pursuit of the most universal community, or the community that would finally be perfectly universal, or the bringing together of truth and community. Where once the law demanded simple obedience, there is now the task of bringing forth community and of finding truth. Now, while these two tasks arise together in the incandescent moment of which I spoke earlier, they pull in opposite directions. The search for what is common tends to gather human beings in the most narrowly unified community possible. Truth, on the other hand, tends to merge with "the universal" and, therefore, to spill over the bounds of every given community. This dialectic between community and truth or universality gives movement and rhythm to the history of the West.

The task or enterprise that I am sketching here is, I think, proper to the West, because these two ideas of truth and community are proper to the West. In any case, it is proper to the West to engage these two together dialectically. Other civilizations—I'm taking a leap here—accept, without flinching, the "beautiful lie" or "noble lie" that no human order can do without if it wants to live and to last. This noble lie consists in saying: "We are the children of the Earth!" or "We are the children of the Sun!" or, as the Japanese used to say, "Our land is the land of the gods." Not so long ago, a Japanese prime minister raised some eyebrows by repeating this timeless formula: "Japan is the land of the gods." In civilizations unlike ours, the truth-status of these propositions is not questioned, not because men there are somehow less capable or less desirous of questioning what is worthy of being questioned, but because the intellectual instruments indispensable to the conduct of this inquiry have not been elaborated for them—or had not been elaborated before the encounter with the West.

The West begins (I cannot avoid these abrupt formulae) when the Greeks question the noble lie of cities and define it as such, that is, when they define it precisely as a "noble lie," which is, as you know, Plato's formula. It is worth saying in passing that Marcel Detienne wastes his immense learning as a Hellenist and anthropologist by trying to deny this obvious point, that is that, from this point of view, the Greeks are characterized by radical innovation and a qualitative superiority relative to other civilizations. Rather than living under the law received from ancestors, the law of the fathers, the Greeks will live in a common world that they produce: they will govern themselves.

The Greeks told each other as many or more stories as other people; they were prodigious story-tellers, but these stories had a different status insofar as the Greeks, by distinguishing *logos* from *mythos*, were able to criticize their myths. I would not say that the Greeks believed less in their stories than the Japanese—who can say?—but only the Greeks *clearly* conceived of a radically different way to say what a human being is other than telling stories. The Greeks taught us that, rather than telling stories, it is possible to consider the *being* of things, the *being* of humans; it is possible to *theorein*, to look at what is with the eye of the mind. The eye of the mind can discover before it a stable and determinate object, which is accessible only to the eye of the mind: the *idea*. In other civilizations, "the wise man has no ideas."

Of course, even in the Greek world, each city remains particular and is even at war with the other cities. But the Greeks, and not only the philosophers, have a very vivid feeling that human nature is manifesting itself among them to an extent inaccessible to other people. The Greeks are the first to expose their nakedness and they take pride in it, in this capacity to show one's nakedness. And it is in civic life that human beings achieve the most explicit self-manifestation. If one considers together all the manifestations of Greek life—the *agora*, sculpture, temples, nudity—everything in Greek life declares: "Here is man!"

Do the Jews participate in this Western heritage? Where do you situate Israel in the dialectic between the particular and the universal?

To be sure, in Jerusalem nudity was not liked at all, and Greek life was not well viewed for that reason, among others. But Jerusalem is not so different from Athens concerning the universal. Of course, the opposition that Leo Strauss famously insisted on between Athens and Jerusalem is radical. On the one hand, there is the deployment of human capacities and confidence in these capacities, culminating in the free philosophic quest. On the other, Jerusalem, there is the experience of divine majesty, the feeling of smallness and unworthiness, and the concern for making one's whole life a life of continual obedience to divine law. All that is true. But Jerusalem is universalist; this is what differentiates Judaism from other non-Western civilizations and places Jerusalem within the Western quest for the universal. Allow me to cite Deuteronomy, when Moses declares: "See, I have taught you decrees and laws as the Lord my God commanded me, so that you may follow them in the land you are entering to take possession of it. Observe them carefully, for this will show your wisdom and understanding to the nations, who will hear about all these decrees and say, 'Surely this great nation is a wise and understanding people.' What other nation is so great as to have their gods near them the way the Lord our God is near us whenever we pray to him? And what other nation is so great as to have such righteous decrees and laws as this body of laws I am setting before you today?" (Deuteronomy 4:5–8) The Law is not given to Israel to belong to her alone, but in order that Zion might be a "light for the nations."

Jerusalem does not represent particularity or particularism. The universalism of Jerusalem is the very meaning of Israel's election. Contrary to what Spinoza will say in manifest bad faith, Israel's election creates a covenant between God and human beings for the benefit of all humanity. To express the meaning of Jerusalem in the language of Athens, since man is by nature a political animal, God can only make himself known to human beings by forming in their midst, or out of their midst, a people that can be His people. Again, the experience of Israel is the means of making known the Creator of humanity to the whole of humanity. Israel is the mediator between humanity and its creator. Needless to say, Israel does not always live up to its vocation; the Bible is, for that matter, largely the chronicle of these failures, but that changes nothing of the nature of Israel's vocation, which is precisely to provide the criterion by which to appreciate these failures. The particularity of Israel is, in this sense, different from the particularity of other civilizations. It is no doubt for this reason that Israel is still at the heart of the life of the world.

But these versions of the universal are never recognized as such by their mediators.

Of course, neither Athens, nor Jerusalem, nor the Christian Church wholly or visibly brings about the fulfillment of humanity: something always goes wrong! As for Athens, there is the obstacle presented by the plurality of cities: how can the universality of *logos* and the plurality of cities be reconciled? There was an attempt to accomplish this by the action of the philosopher-king, or at any rate, by the approximation of the philosopher-king named Alexander. According to Plutarch's interpretation, which I mentioned a moment ago, Alexander, by applying Aristotle's philosophy against the very advice of Aristotle (and I cite Plurarch), "gathered together in a whole all the scattered elements of the world, mixed and recomposed in a great cup of friendship, lives, characters, marriages and customs, and wanted all to see the earth as their fatherland." Alexander brought about the first Western globalization.

As for Jerusalem, things are obviously much complicated by the fact that the mediation of the Chosen People encountered the competition of the mediation of the Christian Church; thus the fate of Israel's mediation has been determined, or in any case, overdetermined, by the fate of Christian mediation. It was as difficult for Jews to understand what Christian mediation could add to Israel's mediation (besides hostility to Israel) as it was for Christians to understand what meaning the Jewish mediation could retain after the coming of the Messiah. What can be said is that Christianity understood itself as the fulfillment of the promise of a Judaism that had become prisoner to its election, or to too narrow an understanding of this election. The Church, which considers itself the new Israel and the true Israel, not only embraces all human beings in principle, but human beings in every condition, as Paul famously said in his *Letter to the Galatians*: "There is neither Jew, nor Greek, nor slave, nor free man; there is neither man, nor woman; for you are all one in Jesus Christ."

To sum up (since we are depicting the history of Europe with the broadest of brush strokes): the first version of Europe takes the form of two modalities of the universal: on the one hand, the Greek, and then Roman Empire, and on the other, the Catholic or universal Church. As is well known, the conflict between the authority of the Empire and that of the Church will be one of the sources of the movement, or perhaps one of the causes of the immobility, of Western Europe in its youth.

After the confrontation between the Empire and the Church, the decisive phenomenon, or one of the decisive phenomena, was obviously the fragmentation of Christianity following the Reformation. What were the consequences of this? These we have already evoked. First, the framework of life, including Christian life, becomes the national framework; and the nation, now confessional, that is, religious, thus gains decisively in authority: henceforth, it is the community *par excellence*. Moreover, as the common denominator of Christian confessions or as the sum of distinct Christian confessions, Christianity undergoes a *diminution capitis* or a qualitative loss of authority. Finally, since Christianity's claim to universality has been damaged, the elaboration of a successor universal is set in motion, a universal exempt from the inevitable particularization that had affected the Church. This new universal, which is expected finally to fulfill the history of universality, is clearly humanity, in the sense of which we were speaking earlier, the sense in which the Enlightenment understood this term.

Here is the ambiguity of this process in which the confessional nation-state reinforces the authority of the national form and, at the same time, the confessional nation-state is affected by Christianity's general loss of authority and by the ascending authority of a new universal. Thus the nations of Europe, after having mediated Christianity in the sixteenth and seventeenth centuries, will strive in the following centuries to mediate the new universal:

humanity. Neither Christianity nor humanity can do without the mediation of a real human community. In European history, the nation was not at all the vehicle of a simple particularism; on the contrary, it was the mediator of the two great universals that Europe has known: the Church's and humanity's. I could add besides that it was also the mediator of the Empire, since the national kings saw themselves as "emperors in their kingdoms."

Good, I will take off my seven-century boots! By calling attention here to certain decisive moments in European history, I have simply tried to bring to light its fundamental source of energy—a source that I call, for lack of a better term, the mediation of the universal, where "mediation" is understood in an active sense. Perhaps "mediatization" would be a better term, but it is no longer available![xi]

Do not other civilizations seek what is common as a support for the universal?

My point is not, of course, to evaluate such immense things as Chinese civilization or Arab-Muslim civilization, or any other. It is clear that each one contains traits that are not only admirable, but traits that make it, in a given important aspect, more satisfying or attractive than Western civilization. And while I know or have some idea of certain accomplishments of these civilizations, I am well aware that I am ignorant of most of them, due to my lack of familiarity and, as it were, intimacy with them. My concern is not to posit some inherent superiority of our civilization. What interests me is this *movement* that has born the West along since its Greek origin, one that aims at once to produce what is common and to seek universal truth—with the tension between these two that I have already indicated. This movement was certainly proper to the West, and it is not certain that, even today, any other great civilization has entirely and without reservation joined the Western movement, a movement in which, since the 19th century, they have all been obliged to participate in some degree. As I have already indicated, these Western accomplishments have their undersides and their pathologies, whether we are talking about the production of the common or the rigorous pursuit of truth. At the time of the French Revolution, for example, the excessive will to produce what is common brought about, according to Constant's formula, "the sacrifice of actual people to the people en masse." And has not this concern for the exact idea, an idea to be held with a perfect sincerity, a concern in which Greek philosophy and Christianity meet, sometimes drifted into the inquisition of intimate beliefs, which is the underside of Western religion?

With these clarifications in mind, I maintain that it seems to me that the other great civilizations are not preoccupied with the requirements of the common or the universal, by the dialectic between truth and community, with the same degree of intensity or clarity. For them, the common tends to be confused with mores and customs, and does not constitute something common to which each person is called to participate and for which political activity takes responsibility.

Not all collective order is political order. Other civilizations, as for that matter European civilization in its earliest forms, are based on the familial order, that is, the order of extended families and thus the power of heads of families. This takes multiple forms: there are clans, tribes, families, and dynasties.

There is something evident and unsurpassable in the familial order because it is rooted in beginnings, in the origin, in "where we come from." Look at how, even in France, the power of fathers of families was still written into the Civil Code until recently. This is, therefore, a dimension of human existence that is never entirely abolished and that must not be, because it belongs to the human condition. But it is true that, whereas other civilizations are based on acceptance of this order of the origin—the familial order, the order of the fathers—the West broke with this fatalism of the familial order. The West shifts permanently, one might say, toward what it will become by producing itself, toward what it can produce itself, that is, what is common. There is truly something singular in this European gesture, in this great task of inventing the common that the Europeans assumed. This means to invent, not as one makes a table, but to invent as one discovers a heretofore unexplored dimension of human life.

Christianity has an ambivalent relationship to the family. Can one say that, following the Greeks, it maintained the rupture with the familial order?

Here, we must distinguish Christianity as such from what actually happened during the Christian centuries. What I call the order of fathers belongs in part to the human condition, as I have said. A man giving the law to his wife, or to his wives, and to his children, according to Homer's formula, which Aristotle cites, concerning the Cyclopes—this is, in short, the first version of human order, a version that still applies for a good part of humanity. The Greeks broke with this order insofar as fathers left the household in order to gather in the public place (if you will allow this shortcut). The establishment of Christianity coincided in part with the disappearance of the civic order. What we call feudal society would be recomposed on the basis of families and heads of families which, despite their bonds of vassalage, did not constitute something common in the proper sense. As I have said, the Church, in its main tendency, would not be favorable to the reconstitution of the civic order—the Greek or Roman order—and would thus find support in the family, with which it will form a close alliance, as the human community most hospitable to the Church's influence. The family was the place of the education of children and of the influence of women, who were more docile or open to the influence of the Church than men. Without going so far as Michelet's fantasies concerning the Woman and the Priest, we can say that the Church consolidated the family by weakening the power of the father. It weakened this power particularly by giving children complete freedom to marry, without deferring to the will of the father. It is clear that, in practice, fathers long maintained great power over the conjugal choices of their children, but the Christian notion of marriage nevertheless broke entirely with the order of fathers: the substance of the sacrament is the very consent of the spouses, the priest himself serving only to witness its validity. Thus, while Christianity does not break as sharply as the Greek city with the familial order, it gently but very profoundly subverts the power of fathers, which is a main element of this order.

There is nevertheless a point on which the Christian rupture was very abrupt: the priests of the Catholic Church are celibate. Thus, a society—the Church—was organized on the suppression of what had everywhere and always been the primary source of collective order, the generative power of males. The priest, as mediator of divine fatherhood, practices a purely spiritual paternity. Contemporary opinion likes to see the celibacy of priests as evidence that the Church is archaic, since the Church is supposed to be the last bastion of "male power." In reality, the celibacy of priests marks the essential rupture between the order of Christian life and the order of familial life. We read in the Gospel: "Whoever does the will of my Father in heaven, he is my brother and my sister, and my mother."

Would not this rupture be even more convincing if women could be priests?

As you know, most Protestant Churches have followed your suggestion, but not the Catholic Church. Why? I am not a theologian, so I proceed very cautiously. In the words of the catechism: by virtue of his consecration, the priest acts "in the power and place of the person of Christ himself." Christ, moreover, chose men to make up the body of apostles, and these have done the same. "The Church considers itself bound by the choice of the Savior himself." This argument, or these arguments, have weight for those who take seriously the notions of revelation and of tradition, which is normally the case of Christians. On the other hand, one might think that Christ's choice was motivated by the social circumstances of his time more than by some essential necessity that the priesthood be reserved to men. It is hard to see an essential link between the priest's ministry and his belonging to the masculine sex.

Setting aside the theological question, one might ask what could be the "anthropological meaning" of such a male exclusivity today, when all other functions have been opened to women. I can see only one possibility. It would have to do with showing that the sexual difference plays an essential role in the "divine plan," and thus in the ultimate sources of the meaning of human life. From the creation of man through his fall to his redemption, sexual difference, in fact, plays a decisive role in the Christian perspective. The way Christianity works is articulated very delicately along the sexual difference, as attested by the place of the Virgin in Catholicism—and this is not so to the same degree for any other religion or philosophy.

Let me then sum up this brief aside in which I should have refused to get involved: I would say that Christianity breaks with the familial order while insisting on the sexual difference.

You will say: the participation of women in the priesthood does not do away with the sexual difference! To be sure, but, by prohibiting all serious public expression of the sexual difference, contemporary society deprives itself of the educative and humanizing role that this difference alone can play.

Let us return to this distinctiveness of the West that has manifest itself since antiquity. What deep marks has it left on us today that other civilizations have more or less not yet taken up?

Other civilizations, or at least certain of them, have more or less taken up most of the inventions upon which the West has built its development and its domination. To take the canonical example: in a few generations, Japan has assimilated the sciences and techniques, the bureaucratic state, and free elections, even though, as you know, the authenticity of Japanese democracy was long doubted. What, then, might be the deep marks, distinctive of the West, which even the Japanese have not yet been able to appropriate? What might these mysterious sources be? Allow me to speculate a bit.

When the Greeks invented the political city (if you will excuse the pleonasm); they discovered at the same time—and, in fact, the two are inseparable—the source of human life, that by which we do what we do and we are what we are, that is, the soul. This discovery comes from philosophy and not from religion, contrary to what many believe. The soul is the principle of life; it lies at the origin of the diverse possibilities of life that make up the unity of human life; it is the synthetic principle of life. And it seems to me that Western history is constituted by the effort to deploy these possibilities of the soul as completely as possible.

Thus formulated, this proposition appears dogmatic, or in any case purely assertoric, which, in fact, it is here. But there are signs, and there are indications, and then there are arguments. One of the signs, for example, that the soul has been discovered or made manifest is when confidence is shown in it—here, again, we find the question of confidence in one's own strength. What does it mean to "have confidence in one's soul"? This means that the soul remains unfailingly our principle of movement, or that we remain ourselves throughout all the adventures that we encounter. Obviously, the most emblematic case is that of Ulysses, who, throughout the infinite diversity of his adventures and the thousand ruses of his enterprise, remains the vigorous and wise man that we recognize from the beginning to the end of his story.

You are suggesting, then, that Ulysses is not simply fluctuating and manifold, but on the contrary, that he has enough confidence in himself, in the stability of his being, to call himself "No One."

In effect you confirm my hypothesis.

But can we base a judgment of such general scope on the personality of a hero of the Homeric epic?

In more general or more radical terms, one might say that all the possibilities of the soul are opened up along with the opening of the soul's most dramatic possibility, that is, the possibility of conversion. Conversion refers not only to religion, though it has a particular meaning in a religious context, but also to philosophy.

What is conversion? Conversion consists in the possibility of becoming completely different while staying the same. It takes great confidence in the soul to accept this possibility and to take up this adventure. I believe that one of the reasons there is so much severity toward people who abandon their religion in certain civilizations that are foreign to the West, is not only due to intolerance, a vice familiar to the West as well, but because this possibility is not really recognized as something possible. It is forbidden because it is impossible! To change one's religion is to lose one's being because the soul has not discovered itself in all its possibilities, and, again, it has not discovered that it can stay the same while becoming altogether different.

I believe this confidence in the strength of the soul is the great power of the West, the pagan West as well as the Christian West. Of course, the soul's philosophic adventure and the religious adventure are quite distinct, but the human source is the same. It is well known that Plato's language in describing this reorientation of the soul toward the true light was used abundantly by Christianity in describing conversion to the true God. Thus, confidence in this inner and invisible principle known as the soul has made Western civilization, at least in its deepest tendency, less subject to received customs and external circumstances.

It is clear that in the possibility of conversion are signs of this confidence and internal freedom. But not converting can also be the result of a choice. How can the manifestation of the soul be judged without searching souls?

There is no question here of searching souls. What I am trying to describe are the possibilities of life that are deployed or that become *visible* in the West. Now, conversion is just such a possibility. It is very different from illumination, from fusion with the Whole, from the "mystical" experiences that one finds in most civilizations, perhaps in all. The main point again is this: it is *myself* who becomes an *other*, an other who is, in principle, better than what I was. Of course, not to convert is also a choice, but the question is, "Is such a choice open? Does it have meaning for me?" Now, it seems to me that this possibility is opened up and analyzed with utmost precision by Greek philosophy, particularly by Plato, and that it is, then, in a way generalized by Christianity, but that it is hardly recognizable in other civilizations. In the Indian path of "renunciation," I cannot recognize the operation of which I am speaking. I welcome correction from someone more learned than myself.

What is the West when it is at full strength? It is a battle, either philosophical or religious, surrounding the soul, its order and its movement. How did a person die—as a philosopher or as a Christian? As I mentioned earlier, specifically Christian intolerance is tied to our idea of the soul as the author of choices and, at the same time, as what is at stake in choices, and these choices are not only decisive for the person concerned but also important for all. The concern underlying inquisitions is tied to this discovery of the powers and of the responsibility of each individual soul.

But it is not only in the choice of philosophy or of religion that the soul discovers itself. It seems to me that modern democracy, which is not eager to talk about the soul, presupposes the development that I have just characterized. What is practically decisive in modern democracy? It is not quite the idea of consent, the idea that the leader's decision must always have, in some measure, the support of the community. Counsels, which are known to many civilizations, aim at unanimity. But democracy, precisely, breaks sharply with the principle of unanimity. People vote, and a difference of one vote produces a winner and a loser. What makes democracy difficult to assimilate in many civilizations is the fact that people who are in power naturally have great difficulty abandoning it. This seems to them absolutely unbearable. Thus, when the result of elections is contrary to their hopes, they try to overturn it or to fix the result. The point is not that these people are particularly tyrannical or especially selfish; it is, rather, that their being is bound up with their position of power and that to lose power is to lose their being. Perhaps I have likened philosophical or religious conversion too abruptly and rapidly to the transfer of political power. But in both cases, there is this virtue proper to the West that makes it possible to stay the same while becoming other. The politician of our democracies says, in short, "I won, that's good! I lost, too bad! But, winner or loser, I am the same. I prefer to be the winner rather than the loser, but I still have the same confidence in my own strength."

I add a final remark: the relationship to work that is proper to the modern market economy presupposes a transformation of the soul that has something to do with what we are talking about. I am not presumed to do the work that my father did, and before him, my father's father. Before each person there is an indeterminate future that he must constitute by an activity he has chosen, and which is his personal contribution to the common prosperity. In the revolutionary formula of "careers open to talent," it is especially the egalitarian aspect that we see. The acceptance of uncertainty is also important; uncertainty for each of us. I do not know what will make up the future, but I have confidence that this future will be constituted by *my* work.

In this sense, Christian-democratic-capitalist America sums up and recapitulates these transformations of the soul that gave the soul this confidence in its own strength. And I maintain that this confidence is distinctive of the West.

At least it *was* distinctive of the West. For we now have to ask whether these possibilities of the soul are not being forgotten or even rejected in the West itself. We might have to say that the first two have been absorbed by the third. The market has tended to become the only realm in which the strength of the soul is manifest. The idea of conversion, whether philosophical or religious, has lost its power since the soul has been crushed underneath the postulate that all choices are of equal value, and that there is no point in striving to become better or to fulfill one's highest possibilities (except . . . with a view to the labor market). To convert is considered an insult to equality, since it implies that one choice of life can be better than another. A person who converts to become better than himself seems to aspire to become better than other people.

There is reason to believe, in any case, that the democratic principle of a transfer of power is now at risk in our societies. We rejoiced unwisely at the weakening of social, political, and ideological passions. We rejoiced unwisely at the "end of class conflict." Today, all parties or groups share more or less the same supply of ideas and "values," give or take a few nuances. There are many causes of this state of things, and I do not claim to possess the key to this development. But we see a growing incapacity in Europe to accept political disagreement and run the risk of electoral choice. The tyranny of political correctness is, by the way, the most striking manifestation of this fear of disagreement. The pre-democratic counsel returns *with a vengeance*[xii]; the public space can now only bear unanimity. "The construction of Europe" is the expression and the result of this slow death of democracy. Europe is being built under the reign of the formula: we have no choice. In fact, no one asks the people their opinion except in order to disregard it. Every citizen of a country of Europe knows that he can shout his lungs out, but the train will not stop. The way in which the French, the Dutch, and the Irish have accepted being dispossessed of the choices they had freely and clearly formulated is very troubling. This might be finally the only argument in favor of European construction such as it is being done for us: our old countries are tired; they no longer have the strength to make choices or even seriously to *envision* true choices. Moaning, but finally *consenting*, they confide their destiny to the Machine that is no more than the sum of their renunciations.

It is ironic, in any case, that Europeans experience such a feeling of satisfaction and moral superiority at the very time they are losing, or rather rejecting, what once constituted the specificity and, yes, the superiority of the West.

In short, according to you, we are no longer capable of posing the ultimate question, "What is man"?

We evoked a moment ago the universal quest which is proper to the West. I have only to follow up on this idea. If all human beings are, of course, equally human beings, then the *question* of man is only posed as such, it is only alive among human beings because the West posed it and kept it alive. And it keeps it alive only insofar as it continues to live politically. As I have said, the political body proper to Europe was the nation, the nation as mediator of universals—the Church and then humanity.

The European Union is not political; it does not mediate: it *blends* in its own eyes with humanity as it moves toward unification. Today, the religion of humanity, which is Europe's religion, prevents the question of humanity from being posed.

In short, European democratic universalism shades into nihilism; it is the fulfillment of nihilism. It consists in saying: Europe is nothing other and wants to be nothing other than pure human universality. It cannot, then, be anything definite; in a very real sense, it wants to be *nothing*, an absence open in every way to the presence of the other; it wants to be nothing itself so that the other, no matter what other, can be everything that it is. In fact, the "others" too often present us with nothing but their obvious right to their own ways, the excellence of their dress, and the truth of their religion. And so we are losing the questioning tradition of the West.

You allude to the fact that civilizations structured by the familial order do not examine their customs, that they do not have what is common to debate as in the political order?

Europe's questioning disposition is, in fact, tied very closely to the political character of European life. From the beginning (and we know that the beginning constitutes more than half of the development), civic life is naturally questioning, because it displays the central question of common life, that is, the question of justice. To be real, the city must have a determinate regime and, in this sense, it presupposes and imposes a certain response to the question of the regime: an oligarchic response, or a democratic response, etc.

At the same time, each regime is haunted by the other regimes, because the interplay between the few, the many, and the one never ceases. Civic life is always a debate on the nature of the city, however confusedly this often happens. This is a debate whose expression is severely circumscribed by actual political life, and a debate that political philosophy will deploy in all its dimensions.

V. The Common and the Universal

From your point of view, it is clear that it is only by seeing things politically that human nature comes to light.

Looking at things politically allows us to see what is proper to humanity because it allows us to see how man deploys his humanity in the city and how he put his humanity to work and makes it visible, as Claude Lefort has said. But human nature is not a "factual condition" that can be described peacefully by keeping one's distance from what is at stake; it is a vocation that is more or less fulfilled and a political and spiritual dynamic that has its own rhythm, that exhausts itself and then is reborn, that is bent and then relaxes, and that is best discovered by diligently tracing our political and spiritual history. And what do we see when we choose to be well attentive?

In the beginning is civic life. Civic life is public life. In a despotic regime, one cannot know what men are doing; we observe them from afar and interpret signs; each person limits his exposure as far as possible, and all eyes are fixed on the impenetrable gaze of the tyrant. In a free regime, on the contrary, human actions are visible, and they are called to be visible; they offer themselves to be seen and are available to be praised or blamed. The free regime brings with it the light that renders actions visible and allows us to judge them. In the language of the Ancients, which always goes right to what is concrete and essential, the motive of civic or republican life is *glory*. The grandeur of paganism is visibility of strength and the exclusive legitimacy of the visible. Humanity wishes to deploy itself wholly in the visible realm, to be entirely visible, that is, worthy of being seen—glorious.

But the limit of paganism lies in the fact that not everything can be rendered visible. Lucretia, raped by the sons of Tarquin, cannot prove in the eyes of others that she did not consent. The pagan tribunal, which praises and blames what it sees, cannot acquit her. So Lucretia kills herself, in a desperate effort to prove what cannot be proven. As Augustine said, she makes herself a criminal in order to prove herself innocent. Cato's suicide, as much as Lucretia's, shows the limits of pagan glory. Cato cannot share the light with

Caesar, who attracts all glory to himself. The glory of each is incompatible with the glory of the other. Cato can preserve his glory only by withdrawing from the visible world, by killing himself.

Christianity overcomes paganism by overcoming the order of glory, the order of the visible. Christianity forbids suicide, but, in Christian ages, it is no longer necessary to kill oneself in order to try to have one's innocence or virtue recognized. The Christian political revolution can be reduced to these words: the testimony of conscience suffices. This testimony suffices because it is equivalent to a certain degree with God's judgment. Neither the woman who is assaulted nor the man who is conquered is forced to disappear. In short, Christian conscience brings an end to the tyranny of the visible.

The Christian order of the invisible reaches its limits, just as did the pagan order of the visible. Recall the two aspects of the Christian notion of conscience. To be good, an action must fulfill two conditions. First, it must be considered as good by the agent; it must correspond to his internal dispositions. This is the wholly invisible part of the estimation of the action; the witness to this is wholly invisible. Second, this action must be objectively good, that is, in conformity with the rules of good action as these are inscribed in natural or divine law. Conscience must judge according to an objectively good rule. But this rule cannot remain invisible. Because it must rule human actions, humans must be made aware of it through legislation and education.

Historically, this rule was promulgated, or at least made explicit and interpreted, by the Christian Church, the visible Christian Church. Thus, the regime of Christian conscience was a mixed regime, a mixture in which the visible and the invisible were difficult to sort out. The visible Church based its visible power, its public power, on the principle of the invisible conscience; it did no more in principle than to make explicit the laws that the tribunal of the conscience followed spontaneously and invisibly. In practice, conscience did not recognize itself in the tribunal of the Church. From this situation arose this ultimately untenable situation in which the Church "forced belief," even though it explicitly recognized that conscience could not be forced. By exercising a kind of quasi-political power, the Church found itself regularly in opposition with the liberating principle it had brought to the world, that of conscience. How to get out of this tension, this incoherence between what is objective and what is subjective in conscience?

Since it is on the objective or objectified part of the rule of conscience that the visible power of the Church rests, the Enlightenment will suppress this objective part, this part susceptible of formulation in a visible rule, or in a law that the political or religious institution intends to make people respect. The Enlightenment will redefine conscience based on its subjective part alone: it is no longer an invisible tribunal, but a sphere closed to the intrusion of all public institutions, even or especially the Church. In this sphere the agent is alone and sovereign. The tribunal of the conscience is replaced by "the rights of the wandering conscience," according to Bayle's formula.

Of course, this redefinition of conscience is accompanied by a redefinition of political order, of visible order. The principle is no longer glory, as in paganism. Nor is it conscience in its at-once subjective and objective rule, as in Christianity. This principle is now the protection of the individual sphere, the protection of rights, of subjective rights. The Christian conscience, reduced to its subjective part and having become the sovereign individual, can enter into a political order that decisively *separates* the invisible (private, subjective) from the visible—the public space, the State, the law. Of course, the sovereign individual *is not* Christian conscience. Indeed, it is in some respect its opposite insofar as it is formed and constituted through the rejection of any objective rule, of any rule that would claim to be valid independently of his consent. It nevertheless results from its metamorphosis, a metamorphosis that is induced by the tension between the visible and the invisible, an insurmountable tension in the Christian regime.

As you know, we are not through with our troubles, since the modern order is also coming up against its limits. The main one is this: what objective order capable of motivating a common action can result from the mere protection of subjective rights? What public order can be built on the protection of private lives alone?

*In this alternation between the invisible and the visible, the private
and the public, you have, in effect, produced a synthetic history of
human freedom . . .*

At least, I would hope to succeed someday in such a venture. Here,
my purpose is especially to try to convey a sense of the tension of
the arc that makes up our history since the Greek city, to show how
this tension between the visible and the invisible is at work in each
of the three great phases of Europe's history and in the passage
from one phase to the next: paganism, Christianity, and democracy
or modern freedom.

The most important point is that the phases of the past, those
we have left behind, never simply disappear. They have reached
their limits, but they remain present and active. How could paganism be completely behind us, when political life as such always unfolds in the visible order and thus can never entirely escape the
perspective or criterion of glory? Similarly, how can Christianity
be simply behind us if our subjective rights, which are so dear to
us, reside in an inner space that was opened up by the Christian
conscience whose laws we have rejected?

Thus, to take up a metaphor first used by Plato, I would compare the West to a succession of three waves, each emerging from
the thrust and the failures of the preceding. This process involves
succession and superposition, for each wave rests on the one that
preceded it, the one it covers but that carries it along. It follows
that, however modern we may wish to be, we cannot be content to
allow ourselves to be carried along by the latest wave. We must,
like Glaucon, swim in deep waters, since beneath us lie in successive
levels the distinct layers of pagan glory, Christian conscience, and
modern rights. The wave that carries us must not make us forget
the waves that carry it. It is up to us to discern, under the mirroring
surface that captivates and comforts us, the different densities and
salinities of the underlying waters. It is up to us to discern that we
are carried and given life by what we think we have long since left
behind.

ENDNOTES

i   Trans. Bergen Applegate.

ii   Cato the younger killed himself in order not to "outlive freedom" after the defeat of Republican troops by Julius Caesar during the battle of Thapsus (46 B.C.).

iii The Raymond Aron Center for Social and Political Studies is a multi-disciplinary center dedicated to political studies within the EHESS.

iv The aristocratic Roman sequence of offices, or path of honorable success.

v   *La raison des nations. Reflections sur la democratie en Europe.* Gallimard, collection « L'Esprit de la cite, » 2006.

vi Fayard, collection "L'esprit de la cite," 2001. Re-edited Gallimard, collection « Tel, » 2004. English translation by Marc A. LePain, *A World Beyond Politics? A Defense of the Nation State* (Princeton, 2006)

vii *Institut d'études politiques de Paris.*

viii English in the original

ix English in the original

x   English in the original

xi The French term "*mediatisation*" is used with reference to modern electronic media.

xii English in the original.

EPILOGUE

The following is a lecture presented June 13, 2014, at the School for Advanced Studies in Social Sciences in Paris, France. It was presented before a conference on themes of Manent's work on the occasion of his retirement from the School.

PIERRE MANENT, "KNOWLEDGE AND POLITICS"

The question I wish to pose stands without preliminary remarks: what is to be done? This is a question for each and for all, for the human being taken by himself and for the person in association with others. To pose the question "What is to be done?" is to deliberate. We deliberate concerning things that are up to us and that we can bring about. (*Nicomachean Ethics*, 1112 a 31) Who, then, is this "we" who deliberate and bring about? We do not deliberate concerning all human things. For example, Aristotle observes, no Lacedaemonian deliberates on the best form of government for the Scythians. (*NE*, 1112 a 28–29) I start with this observation from the Boss, from which we will see arise not only Aristotle's political science or practical philosophy, but also our science and our philosophy—our science that is not really political, but rather social, and our philosophy that is not really practical, that is, that does not quite know what to do with the question, "What is to be done?" In fact, instead of questioning what action is to be done, we prefer to explain or to understand action that has already been done, that is thus wholly determined, or else approve a future action that is entirely indeterminate but included among our rights. On the one hand, we have the science of action to be done, and on the other, the science of action already done attached to a philosophy of what might be done.

No Lacedaemonian deliberates on the best form of government for the Scythians. The best form of government, the political regime, is the object of deliberation par excellence, one can say, because it conditions all subsequent deliberations, private as well as public, and, of course, citizens deliberate concerning the form of government only of their city. Let us consider more closely Aristotle's example. The Scythians, owing to their distance from Sparta, maintain as it were no significant relations with them. But would the Spartans be just as indifferent to the political regime of the Scythians if Scythia were near Lacedaemonia? In any case, we must wonder why Aristotle had to go to Sparta to find someone who would not deliberate concerning the Scythian regime. This is no doubt because he could not have written: no Athenian deliberates concerning the best form of government for the Scythians. Whereas Sparta was indeed ignorant of philosophy, and especially of political philosophy, Athenian philosophers since Socrates had asked themselves, and thus had deliberated, concerning the best form of government in general, but also concerning the best form according to the diversity of circumstances, including therefore the best form for the Scythians. In fact, Aristotle mentions the Scythians twice in the *Politics*, when he is criticizing cities and peoples who exaggerate the value of war and domination. (1324 b 11, 17) Thus he is concerned with their political regime; he in a way deliberates on their behalf, if not with them. To be sure, this questioning, which involves political science, is not the same thing as civic deliberation, but it is not as foreign to it as the Spartans are to the Scythians, since Aristotle's very purpose— in the *Politics* quite evidently, but also in the *Nicomachean Ethics*—is to clarify the deliberations of citizens, no matter the city to which they belong, in order to improve their political regime, whatever the type of regime, even in the case of a tyranny.

With this observation, as if in passing, concerning the Lacedaemonian who does not deliberate concerning the best form of government for the Scythians, Aristotle draws our attention to the strange character of the science he is laying out. He generally divides the things of the world into two major categories: those that do not depend on us, and those that do. But "things that depend on us" can be understood in two ways. They can depend on "us," understood as concrete and determinate, as for example, the regime and more generally the actions of the city of Sparta depend upon the Spartans. Or they can depend on an indeterminate "us," referring to human things, and particularly human actions, insofar as they depend on human beings in general. By setting forth a political science, or a practical philosophy, Aristotle implies that there is a science of human actions in general, a science of *agenda*. As a practitioner of this science, Aristotle is capable of clarifying the deliberation and the action of a human group just as far removed as the Scythians are from the Spartans, or, indeed, one further removed. Thus practical science deliberates where it does not act. It proposes to accomplish a task that seems impossible, since it consists in treating things that do not depend on us as if they depended on us.

Aristotle thus does not conceal the strange character and the precarious status of the science he is founding. Whereas there is no science but of what is general and no action that is not concrete and determinate, the science he is founding is to be a science of action in general, that is, a science capable of determining what concrete action the acting human being should produce, and not therefore a general action or an action in conformity with some general rule, but a determinate action appropriate to the characteristics of the agent and the circumstances of the action. If this science were to prove impossible, or if we lost confidence in this possibility, then we would find the things of the world laid out in a very different way: instead of being divided between things that do not depend on us and things that depend on us because they depend on human action, they would be divided between those things that depend directly or immediately on us and those things, whether natural or human, that do not depend on us directly. We would then say, to return to Aristotle's example: insofar as they act, all human beings are like the Lacedaemonian who does not deliberate concerning the best government for the Scythians. If we lose confidence in the possibility of a science of deliberation, then we will all be Spartans, deliberating exclusively concerning our regime, concerning our action. What then will become of the Scythians, the Persians, the others in general? Their actions, having ceased to belong to the set of things that depend on us, will become a part of those that do not depend on us; they will become a part of nature, or at least of things that we look at as we look at natural things. We will all be Spartans, which is to say not only that we will deliberate exclusively concerning our own affairs, but also that we will not see others as deliberating—the only deliberation that we would know would be what we experience concretely, that is, our own. Now, if we do not see others as deliberating because we have no knowledge of deliberation in general, then the deliberative character of our own practical attitude is obscured. Our relation to our own action can no longer be based on deliberation. Thus, if Aristotle's enterprise were vain, if there were no science of deliberation, then knowledge of human things would be divided up or dismembered between the point of view of one who effectively acts and the point of view of one who looks at human things as he looks at things that do not change and are not the object of deliberation. Knowledge of human things would be divided up or dismembered between the point of view of the agent and that of the knower. If the science of deliberation were shown to be impossible, or if we lost confidence in its possibility, then we would come to treat things that depend on us as if they did not, and to act on things that depend on us as if they were not the object of science.

This is no imaginary scenario, and we can set aside the conditional tense. We are in fact Spartans, insofar as we have indeed lost confidence in the possibility of a science of deliberation, a science of human action. We can debate the timing and the causes of this loss of confidence, but what seems beyond doubt is that our whole organization of the intellect, as well as our political organization, is in a way based on this loss of faith or is a response to this loss of faith. The immense deployment of the human sciences, which is inseparable from the immense deployment of the institutions of modern politics, is conditioned by the certainty that there is no science of human action, no science of the *agendum*. There are only, on the one hand, the science of *acta*, that is, of things that have been done and are thus in the past, and, on the other, the theory of approved actions, or a philosophy of rights. The science of history is the mother of the human sciences; it treats all actions as if they were in the past, as if they stood before us and did not depend on us, as if they did not depend on deliberating and acting human beings but on causal relations grasped by theoretical reason.

The question whether there is or is not a rigorous science of human action, and of what such a science, if it exists, would consist, depends strictly on the way we understand human action. Let us recall briefly the way Aristotle understands the mechanism of human action, which will bring out the way we understand it and make it clear why for him there is a science of action, and not for us. Once we have posited the purpose of our action (*NE,* 112 b 15), he says, we consider the means by which we will bring it about. Action is the object of a specific science because deliberation is a kind of search or even calculation—the search for or calculation of means. Aristotle seems to attach the first importance to the purpose we posit, but this purpose is not relevant to action until deliberation has found the means and the agent has located the principle of action in himself, in the directing part of himself, since this is the part that chooses. (1113 a 5–7) The purpose is effectively posited only when one has begun to choose the means and to put them to work. Now these means, which vary infinitely with the attendant circumstances and instrumentalities, are nonetheless essentially reducible to a limited number: insofar as practical science strictly understood is concerned, these means present themselves according to a coherent and stable structure in all human actions, a structure formed by the four cardinal virtues. Whenever human beings act, the search for means proceeds by determining the appropriate proportions of courage, temperance or moderation, justice and prudence. Compared with the strength and stability of this basic structure, which is recognizable in all climates and in all human groups, the diversity of human things, their infinite variety, is only a display of insubstantial differences. In any case, if we have the right to speak of humanity as a species sharing a common nature, this is because of this pattern of practical virtues, by which we recognize a courageous and just person in the human being born in the most distant and apparently most different latitude. Should we therefore dismiss the diversity of human customs, which has held, and one might say monopolized, the attention of scholars from Montaigne to Montesquieu, and from Montesquieu to contemporary ethnology, leaving humanity surprised and awed before the spectacle of its own diversity? In any case, diversity appears as the most significant modality of the human phenomenon only if human action is considered mainly in its declared purposes rather than being recognized in its actual means. Diversity becomes primary only when we reduce action to its first and lesser half, the half that consists in "positing the purpose," that is, manifesting a wish or producing an image. This half of action is not really an action, and we see evidence of this in the fact that the diversity of human things manifests itself above all in the domains of human life that have the least to do with action. It is not only because of their interest in what is risqué that Montaigne and Montesquieu enjoy displaying the diversity of sexual and familial customs; it is because these customs, as well as religious customs for that matter, have much less to do with human action than with imagination. On the other hand, as soon as we consider the way a human group governs itself, as soon as we examine its political regime or deliberate on its form of government, then the constancy and, as it were, the monotony of the motives of human action come to the fore. It is always a matter of prudently bringing together the few and the many, justice and moderation, the virtues and arts of peace and those of war. If Americans and members of the Taliban focus on the diversity of their familial and religious customs, they will see each other as very different. But if they seriously negotiate a political transition, they will have no difficulty understanding each other, if not necessarily agreeing.

It might be said that these remarks presuppose an emphasis on the political dimension of human life to the detriment of its other domains, an emphasis that must be considered arbitrary, even if we sympathize with it. Why would an understanding of the political regime be more illuminating than the elementary structures of kinship or the mutual dependence of the religious and the social? One might thus object that all I am doing is extending the "political values" of the Greek city, or more generally the ancient city, well beyond its expiration date. But this objection presupposes what is to be proved, namely, that the difference between times is stronger than the continuity of human political experience. In any case, the word "value," employed in this context, sheds no light on the matter. Instead, it prevents us from thinking through action because it tends to reduce action to a static position. One can say, if one insists, that value is the purpose of action, but this is to presuppose that "value" can exist as simply posited, that it can exist independently of the means sought through deliberation. Value is the end without means, and thus it is not even an end, but at most a wish. It is the lovely but confused image of a possible action, which amounts to little unless deliberation concerning means has been set in motion. Since value is subject to the manifold of representation, the variety of values is infinite, whereas the number of actual motives of action, as we have emphasized, is actually quite limited. And since the political order is based on ongoing deliberation and action, without which it would immediately cease to be, it consists in the ceaseless setting to work of actual motives for action according to the pattern of the cardinal virtues. Thus the primacy of politics is by no means the result of an arbitrary choice of values by the Greeks and the Romans, but something that belongs to the human condition itself. The political order is the order of human life, which can in no way rest content with declaring values, since it is least able to escape the obligation to find the means. One who governs is par excellence one who deliberates concerning means. We have seen, moreover, that the inflation of values is proportional to the weakness of deliberation and the exhaustion of action. Therefore, the science of action is not dependent on an arbitrary valorization of political life; it seeks, rather, I dare say, action where it is most complete, which, moreover, leads it to appreciate the importance of the political regime, even in what drives familial and religious organization. Human motives are accessible to clear understanding only when they produce an action that manifests itself visibly in the public space, rather than a movement of the soul that finds completion in feeling or imagination.

I have yet to consider what is no doubt the strongest objection against the propositions that I am here setting forth. If this science of action to be done is so tied to the pattern of practical life provided by the motives and the virtues, and if this pattern is essentially stable and can be found to be at work in all human groups, then why have we renounced this science of action? Yet we have not only renounced it but have rejected it, and the greatest minds over a number of centuries have again and again produced arguments for rejecting the science of *agenda* in favor, as we have seen, of a science of *acta*, for rejecting political or practical science in favor of the science of history, the mother of the human sciences. We must have some solid reasons for this rejection. The Moderns must have some solid reasons. Where shall we look for them?

We confront the following enigma: The Moderns have undertaken great actions, ever greater actions, even as they renounced ever more completely the science of action in favor of the science of history, the science of action to be done in favor of the science of action already done. This paradox suggests that the practical framework had been struck by some unprecedented uncertainty. Something prevented us from orienting ourselves according to the *agendum*. We felt a greater and greater need to see human history before our eyes, to look at it as something accomplished, in order to know what we had to do. This is the deepest motive of the idea of progress, which grounds our perspective on human things. But again, why is this so?

The answer that seems to me most plausible is not new and has been given by countless authors, both historians and philosophers; but this near-unanimity is of little help because everything depends on how this answer is understood. The answer I have in mind is the one that says that what drives European development as distinctively European lies originally in the intervention of Christianity. As I just said, this thesis comes in so many versions that, considered in itself, it has little meaning. I will specify it in the following way: the essence of the Christian proposition understood as an historical factor is that it introduces something deeply troubling, a problem that proved insurmountable, in the practical framework, the arrangement of human virtues and motives. It addresses humanity with demands of unprecedented radicality. In particular, it presents a demand that endangers the natural framework of motives and virtues, that is, the political association. It endangers the political framework of human life by requiring human beings to love their enemies. One must ask how this exorbitant requirement could ever have been put forward, understood and propagated, but in any case, it represented a radical modification of the relationship between the political order and the religious order. Up until the irruption of the Christian proposition, the religious association was not distinguished from the political association; the gods were only an institution of the city, an institution that was considered open to negotiation and was sometimes, in fact, quite badly mistreated. The rewards and punishments distributed by the gods belonged essentially to this world. This is still the case for the Jewish religion, whose prayer knows no other reward than length of days and a numerous posterity. With the Christian Church, religion becomes entirely distinct from the political order; it leaves behind the radical dependence that tied it to the political order in order to attain an essential independence. It lives, henceforth, from a principle that is not nature, in particular not man's political nature, namely charity, or obedience to the commandment to love one's enemies.

Of course, the structure of virtues and motives remained what it is by nature. It goes without saying that Christians continued firmly to hate their neighbors. The Church, as the organ and vehicle of the Christian proposition, would not avoid intimate involvement in the political order. It would sometimes seem to be on the point of being reabsorbed by natural motives, either through its claims to rule the political order itself, or because, in the ancient manner, whether pagan or Jewish, it functioned as a complement to the political order. Nevertheless, to whatever degree natural human motives pervade or, if you will, corrupt the church, it continues to escape the political order in its commandment to love one's enemies, a commandment that maintains its mysterious power of intimidation, however little it is followed in practice. That this is so is evident in the fact that the most vigilant enemies of Christianity, from Machiavelli to Nietzsche, keep conceiving more and more extreme ways to deliver humanity from such a penetrating, and in their eyes degrading, commandment.

A commandment so contrary to nature would never have captivated men's ears, and sometimes their hearts, if it had not been formulated by an agent who, as mediator between human beings and God, freely took upon himself all of human enmity. It is the figure of Jesus Christ that renders the ever-imminent reabsorption of the religious association into the political association impossible. It is the words he spoke that can be said to command the respect of the most powerful motives of nature, however little power they have to change the actual conduct of human beings. Joined to the sacrifice that seals them, these words guarantee that enmity has been overcome. In more immediately theological terms, the mediation of the Son, which is indispensable to reach the Father—the mediation of he in whom all enmity meets its death—prevents the Father from being enlisted in the service of the city and prevents Christianity from producing a "political theology." Carl Schmitt will be able to imagine a supposedly Christian "political theology," a theology that, since it is intended as specifically "political," commands the hatred of one's enemies, but only by injecting enmity within the Trinity itself. But again: *Gesta Dei per Francos, Gott mit uns*, God bless America—as long as Christians are human beings, they will continue to relate to their religion at least in part in a natural way, that is, politically; but the doctrine of the Trinity will always preserve the substantial independence and essential irreducibility of the Christian proposition.

The questions I have raised would, of course, require a much more precise treatment, but I must nevertheless pursue my argument. Again, my concern is with the debate between the science of action to be done and that of action already done, between political science and the science of history. For many, the irruption of Christianity obliges us to adopt the historical point of view, since this irruption introduced a radical change in one's perspective on human action; it defines a difference between historical periods that cannot be understood within the perspective of man's political nature, which must be essentially unchanging. I do not think we will better understand what has happened by understanding it as "history." Of course, we can say that Christianity came after paganism and that today we live in a post-Christian era. The problem with this history is not that it is inaccurate, but that it is History, and that we look at is as if were sitting in a panoramic cinema watching the great film of the history of humanity. But this is a luxury we cannot afford. We cannot look at the person who is deliberating as if he had always already deliberated, as if he were a thing that did not change, or as if his action did not depend on himself. Action stood before Pericles, it stood before Paul of Tarsus, and it stands before us. The question is to know how we can put the city's reasons to work, and thus what is our courage, what is our moderation, what is our justice, what is our prudence. And the question is further to know if we hear the commandment to love our enemies, and how we understand it. All, or almost all, of today's dominant representations of history presuppose that history has made the choice for us, and that it is not up to us to act because we no longer have a choice, because things were decided long ago. In short, things were decided by *no one*, but they were decided. We are rights-bearing individuals who have nothing left to do in this world or in the next but claim our rights.

Without underestimating my persuasive power, I suspect that few of you would concede that the choice stands before us as it did before Pericles or Saint Paul. In any case, for many of our contemporaries, there is a movement in modern societies that is visible enough, that carries us along powerfully enough and has done so for long enough that we can say confidently enough that things were indeed decided without us and prior to us, and that we can, without much bad conscience, say goodbye to Aristotle and to the Gospels. My answer to this is that this movement that seems irresistible is not nearly as strong as it seems, or that it draws its strength more and more from a refusal to choose, or from a number of such refusals, that cannot go on indefinitely.

To sum up as synthetically as possible the human problem as a practical problem, I am inclined to say that it is always a question of linking words with actions, and vice versa. In the city, where the motives of future actions are persuasively expounded and reasons are given for past action, words accompany the visible action where the weight of things resides. The Christian proposition favors words or, in any case the Word. To be sure, the validity of Christian words is witnessed by actions, by works, but there is also a Word before all action, a Word that the Christian never succeeds in attaining. There is, for example, the extremely problematic proposition that one might become a eunuch for the kingdom of heaven. This word is scandalous, like the commandment to love one's enemies, as we have seen. In any case, the Christian world lived under the authority of intimidating words that were difficult to dismiss but just as difficult to link with common familial and political actions, with "Christian marriage" and the "Christian nation." A certain stability would thus be sought in the confessional nation and the politically prudent State that, after having imposed an orthodoxy, turned in the direction of neutrality or of secularism which we know so well. But what matters for us here is rather the instability of the Word in general and of the words that sought a place between the Church and the State, the State and the nation, the State and society. What was continually sought was the link between the Word or the words and action. The solution was found in the representative regime, which established the connection between the social word and governmental action. Representative government draws its life from the social word, and the neutral State guarantees that it takes shape and does so freely.

Representative government was an admirable accomplishment, but it was affected by a serious weakness. The problem is not only that representation is inherently problematic, that is, that it is almost always found to be disappointing, since those who are represented naturally tend to judge that they are ill-represented by their representatives. The problem is a more radical one, namely, that the representative regime tends to obscure the site and the nature of action. Where does one really act, and who is it that acts? Where, in truth, is the acting human being? Is he to be found in civil society or in the state? Marx thought that this uncertainty and this division were untenable, and the meaning of the revolution as he first envisioned it was to unify the site of action, to bring action to the unity of its site, such that the actor might speak according to his own words and act according to his speech. Representative government calls forth the desire for a return to the unity of the political community beyond the division between representative and represented, and this "revolutionary" desire is nothing if not natural. As Marx once again expressed this unforgettably, the modern citizen, divided between civil society and the State, is just as torn apart and perplexed as the Christian who hesitates between earth and heaven. This, by the way, is why I am not convinced by interpretations of totalitarianism that see it as an anachronistic reversion to a holistic society in a world that has already seen the rise of individualism. I see in it instead an effort finally to connect word firmly to action so as to deliver both from the uncertain and demoralizing oscillation that is proper to the representative regime. It is precisely the role of ideology to connect all possible actions in a determinate and closed whole of words. And it is the role of the ideological party to bring word and action together explicitly, and even emphatically and pedantically. Of course, this connecting is arbitrary and violent, since the same word justifies opposing actions, according to circumstances; it is inherently dishonest, but the aim of bringing the uncertainty of representation to an end responds to a natural desire of the political and speaking animal. After all, what we call political correctness, which of course is not to be confused with totalitarian force, is also a discipline of speech that attempts to respond to the current malaise of the representative regime, a regime in which one no longer knows who represents what or whether or not a political body is being represented. We have rejected the totalitarian temptation, but we no longer know what is the point of our deliberation; we no longer know to what end nor for whom we deliberate, nor even if we deliberate. So we require ourselves to speak in such a way that we name the *other* only to emphasize the he is the *same*. Our "we" is left indeterminate in an operation of unlimited *identification* with every *other*, an identification in words that takes the place of any effort at active and concrete association, which we have renounced.

Aristotle's question has come back with an acuteness that Aristotle could not have imagined. For whom are we deliberating? For whose best form of government are we deliberating? For France's? For that of the Euro Zone? Or of the European Union? Of today's European Union, or the European Union of tomorrow? If we no longer know for whom we deliberate, then we cannot actually deliberate and we leave behind the domain of action properly understood. The political and spiritual movement of the effacing of borders into which we have put all our virtue has led us to a point at which we have deprived ourselves of the conditions of deliberation, not by the violence of a tyrannical power, but by a voluntary suspension of our active power, a deactivation of the *ergon* proper to the human being as citizen. To put the world in order, we think, no longer resides in the activity of the cardinal virtues but in abandonment to the contagion of the same and, in short, in the organization of our passivity. Adaptation to the necessities of globalization is the modest and thus persuasive name of this immense disarmament.

Under this ostensibly utilitarian injunction, an immense spiritual power has arisen that influences every movement of the soul with more authority than the Church of Rome ever exercised. Anyone who expresses the modest desire to continue to speak and to teach in his maternal language, which might be French, for example, finds himself beaten down by a storm of blunt arguments— China is thrown in along with America, the law of comparative advantage and Shanghai's economic ranking; in a word, the whole world is heaped on your shoulders, and you cannot bear the burden. Those who speak in the name of the world are obviously irrefutable. The only thing they are forgetting is that necessity can be a rule of action only if this action has a specific goal and aims at a good that is in itself worthy of choice. For the necessities of globalization to provide an actually useful criterion, we would have to form a deliberative community capable of taking account of these necessities in the pursuit of an end desirable in itself. But globalization as it is now conceived by the European civil religion consists in preventing anything that might lead to the crystallization of a deliberative community, either national or involving several European nations.

I did not underestimate the psychic satisfactions implicit in what I call the deactivation of our powers. After all, those who have put their faith in the contagion of sameness have no enemy either to fight or to love. There is no more need to question the relation between the political and the Christian virtues, since one is relieved of both. But this is an act of faith, a wager. And so it is, after all, an act. Our action consists in the strange suspension of action. We have confidence in the fact that our inaction will become more and more irresistible for ourselves and for those around us. I believe on the contrary that the extension of the domain of our passivity—the "broadening" of the domain of our passivity—will only make the moment of decision more dangerous, the moment when internal and external disorder will render the *definition* of the framework of deliberation and of action more imperious and, in truth, necessary.

We find ourselves settled within this mutilated conception of practical life that understands this life as the positing of values. We posit values and we look at the facts. We posit values with an ever greater indifference toward the facts. And we command ourselves to obey more and more the facts that press down upon us more and more. Our faith in the contagion of sameness postulates a world that puts up no resistance. Our science of globalization postulates a world to which we cannot put up any resistance. But it is when we act that we experience the world's resistance and, at the same time, that we resist the world. It is this negotiation with the world that the cardinal virtues administer. It is through them that the influence of the world and our influence on the world come together. And it is only in a community of deliberation and of action that this coming together, which is always precarious, can happen. Thus, today as in the past, and today much more than in the past, the question of actions to be done lies before us, and political or practical science is always, or is now again, the first of the human sciences.

Index